Merit and Moses

Merit and Moses

A Critique of the Klinean Doctrine of Republication

ANDREW M. ELAM,
ROBERT C. VAN KOOTEN,
and RANDALL A. BERGQUIST

Foreword by William Shishko

WIPF & STOCK · Eugene, Oregon

MERIT AND MOSES
A Critique of the Klinean Doctrine of Republication

Wipf and Stock
An Imprint of Wipf and Stock Publishers
199 W. 8th Ave., Suite 3
Eugene, OR 97401

www.wipfandstock.com

ISBN 13: 978-1-62564-683-5

Manufactured in the U.S.A.   07/21/2014

Contents

Foreword

During my years at Westminster Theological Seminary, Philadelphia (1976–79), I became aware of the sharp divergence that Dr. Meredith Kline had with Professor John Murray on the subject of the covenants. For Murray, the succession of covenants in the Bible (including the Mosaic covenant) was "a sovereign administration of grace and promise."[1] For Kline, law rather than grace was foundational. The Mosaic covenant in some sense included a "works principle" which was, in Kline's mind, essential to preserve the distinction between law and gospel.[2] Therefore, the real issue was the nature of the gospel. It was shocking to hear Dr. Kline say publicly, "John Murray's view of the covenants makes the gospel mush."[3]

Now fast forward to the present. The volume *The Law Is Not of Faith*,[4] a collection of essays dealing with issues related to works and grace in the Mosaic covenant, was published in 2009. With contributions largely from faculty members and others associated with Westminster Theological Seminary, California, the book developed and expanded Meredith Kline's ideas regarding the Mosaic covenant. It popularized the view that the Mosaic covenant was, in some sense, a republication of the covenant of works. Since then a minor torrent of articles, interchanges, and debates have

1. See Murray, *Covenant of Grace*, 31.

2. See Kline, *Kingdom Prologue*, 352–53.

3. Spoken by Dr. Kline in his Zechariah class, Westminster Theological Seminary, ca. 1977/78; heard firsthand by the author.

4. Estelle et al., *The Law Is Not of Faith.*

fueled the controversy—a controversy in which, it is claimed, the very integrity of the gospel is at stake.

Which brings us to the study before you.

The brothers who have produced this book have helped us immeasurably in getting a hold of contemporary teaching on this subject (much of it coming from Westminster in California). Growing out of a discussion and debate in the Presbytery of the Northwest of the Orthodox Presbyterian Church, this book is an exposé of the way Meredith Kline's ideas about the Mosaic covenant have been developed by modern proponents of the "republication theory," i.e., that the Mosaic covenant is, in some sense, a republication of the Adamic covenant of works.

I found the study to be both fascinating and distressing.

Building on ideas offered in some of Meredith Kline's later writings, I was fascinated to learn how some modern proponents of the republication view have developed a two-tiered approach to understanding the Mosaic covenant. On one level, there is a principle of grace, but, on the other level, there is a principle of works. As the writers of this book show, this leads to a bifurcated form of spirituality for the old covenant people of God. This hardly seems to fit with historic understandings of piety in its Old Testament form.

I was distressed to read how some modern proponents of the republication view now speak of a form of "merit" in the obedience of Israelites to the Mosaic covenant. One is at pains to find anything like this in Protestant theology. Further, as the study shows, the "republication view" can only by smoke and mirrors be made to fit with the doctrine of the covenants as developed in the Westminster Standards or, for that matter, with any other Reformed doctrinal standard. This is distressing, indeed. The propagation of these views is something that should deeply concern all churches committed to Reformed doctrinal standards.

And keep in mind that this study brings to light the views of those who hold that *not* to accept the republication teaching in some form or other is to pave the way for serious erosion of the gospel. The editors of *The Law Is Not of Faith* make this patently clear when they write, "In short, the doctrine of republication is *integrally connected to the doctrine of justification. . . .a misunderstanding of the Mosaic economy and silence on the works principle embedded there will only leave us necessarily impoverished in our faith. We will see in only a thin manner the work of our Savior.*[5] In a similar vein, one of the endorsers of that volume notes: "This anthology argues that the Mosaic covenant in some sense replicates the original covenant with Adam in the garden, and that this notion is neither novel to *nor optional for* Reformed theology."[6] Those within the Reformed community should be justly concerned that a view which begs for tolerance and understanding actually carries with it a conviction that to reject the view is to actually impoverish or even undermine our view of the work of Christ and the gospel. If you read the study before you for no other reason, read it realizing that this is what at least some "republication" advocates believe. The issue is not to be taken lightly.

I am thankful that the authors of this book have raised important biblical, historical-theological, confessional, systematic-theological, exegetical, and eminently practical issues advanced by modern expressions of the "republication" view. I laud the authors for pursuing these things in the church, and not in inflammatory blogs. I greatly appreciate their thorough research in materials most of us will not have the time to read. I am thankful for the gracious spirit with which they write and treat the brothers whom they are critiquing. And, most of all, I welcome their bringing to our attention things that must be studied and debated within the context of historic Reformed orthodoxy.

For now: *Tolle lege!* Take and read this rich study. Let the reader judge whether the current "republication" views are in accord with both the Scriptures and the historic confessional standards of Reformation Protestantism. Like the noble Bereans, may we "examine the Scriptures" whether these things are so (Acts 17:11).

William Shishko, Pastor
Orthodox Presbyterian Church, Franklin Square, NY

5. Ibid., 19, emphasis mine.
6. Ibid., book endorsements, inside front cover, emphasis mine.

Preface

How did three graduates of Westminster Seminary California, former students of Meredith G. Kline, come to write a book critical of his system of theology? After all, we are all fellow ministers in the Orthodox Presbyterian Church and at one time believed and taught many of the things he taught us. As fellow ministers in the Orthodox Presbyterian Church, all three of us have great appreciation for much of what we learned from our late professor, though we now see clearly serious flaws in his formulation of the covenants.

In the spring of 2011, we became more aware that Professor Kline's view of the Mosaic covenant was at the heart of a growing debate about the doctrine of the republication of the covenant of works. In 2009, a book was published entitled *The Law Is Not of Faith: Essays on Works and Grace in the Mosaic Covenant* (*TLNF*). It vigorously advocated Kline's view of republication as the historical Reformed position. This book contained articles by men whom we respect both as professors and writers, including some who were our fellow classmates at seminary. The same was also true of those writing critical reviews or articles on the book. Some of these were men under whom we had studied, along with others we knew personally. We had high regard for men on both sides of this growing debate.

We realized that we needed to get a better understanding of the theological issues involved. What was this debate really about? As we read the introduction to *The Law Is Not of Faith*, it became clear that the editors of the book believed the doctrine of republication as taught by Dr. Kline was not just a side issue in Reformed theology—rather it was essential to a clear understanding of justification. They challenged their readers to consider whether their own teaching and preaching could maintain the doctrine of justification and a proper view of our Savior without holding to their view of the doctrine of republication. They were hopeful that their book would "encourage and catalyze discussion about what we believe are important issues for the doctrine and life of the church."[1]

Thus, the three of us chose to take up their challenge. We began to study *The Law Is Not of Faith* carefully, as well as various critical reviews. We then turned to the original sources and other writings referenced in the book, as well as the creeds of the church and, above all, the Scriptures. As we studied, we slowly became more and more troubled by what the book was setting forth as biblical and confessional. As ministers in the OPC, we have an obligation to speak up if there are teachings in our denomination that are potentially in opposition to our confessional Standards. We debated how best to do this. After careful consideration, we determined to present an overture to our presbytery requesting that the General Assembly of the OPC form a study committee to examine these teachings. At its April 2012 meeting, the presbytery of the Northwest determined not to vote on our overture, but to refer it to a special committee of four men who were instructed to assist the presbytery in its study of the issue of republication of the covenant of works.

The present volume is our contribution—among the contributions of others—to the work of our presbytery in studying these theological matters. As you read this book, keep in mind that it is designed so that each chapter can be carefully read and digested. For this reason, we acknowledge that there is some redundancy, especially the overlapping discussion of the ideas of merit and justice in the Republication Paradigm of chapters 7 and 11. Nevertheless, we felt that the repetition is necessary because these chapters

---

1. Estelle et al., *The Law Is Not of Faith*, 20.

focus on the heart of the issue. Thus, they require the most careful reflection and analysis.

At its September 2013 meeting, the Presbytery of the Northwest (OPC) held a pre-presbytery conference on the doctrine of Republication and voted to ask the 2014 General Assembly of the OPC to establish a study committee to examine these teachings. We hope and pray that this volume will assist the reader in examining the contemporary "Klinean" doctrine of republication that is a growing cause for concern in our denomination, as well as others. May the Triune God grant peace, purity, and unity in our presbytery, our denomination, and the Reformed churches with whom we are united.

We would like to take this opportunity to express our sincere thanks to the respective congregations we serve in Port Angeles, Oak Harbor, and Kent, Washington, for their prayers and encouragement in our labors, and to Jan Shreve for her extra assistance in preparing the manuscript for publication. We are especially grateful to God for—and appreciative of—our families, and their loving, faithful support and encouragement throughout this project.

Andrew Elam, Robert Van Kooten, and Randall Bergquist

March 2014

Introduction

The publication of *The Law Is Not of Faith* (2009) produced no small stir in the Presbyterian and Reformed world. Reviews were written and further theological discourse has ensued. What is all the controversy about? The concerns are focused on the book's central thesis, namely, that the Mosaic covenant was to be considered *in some sense* a republication of the Adamic covenant of works. In theological shorthand, this view is often referred to as the *doctrine of republication*. While this view can take several different forms (even in *The Law Is Not of Faith*), the controversy has become focused on a specific version of republication articulated by the late Professor Meredith G. Kline and more recently by others. This view involves more than what is traditionally taught in Reformed circles, namely, that the moral *law* given to Adam was *reaffirmed—summarized* and *republished*—at Sinai.[1] In the version propounded by Professor Kline (hereafter, Klinean), the nation of Israel is viewed as undergoing a merit-based probation with respect to their retention of temporal blessings in the promised land. This probationary arrangement echoes or reenacts the arrangement first made with Adam, and is analogous to the original covenant of works. More than republishing the *same law* that Adam was given, the *covenant of works itself* was republished *in some sense* at Mt. Sinai. In this construction, Israel becomes a new Adam figure in her national capacity (a "corporate Adam," as the defenders of this view express it). In the original covenant of works, Adam was

---

1. Strimple, "Westminster Confession of Faith," 4.

1

required to fulfill the stipulation of the covenant in order to merit eternal life at the hand of God.[2] In the Klinean republication view of the covenant of works under Moses, Israel was also called to fulfill the stipulations of the covenant through her national obedience in order to merit the retention of temporal blessings of the land. Thus, in this view, the obedience of Old Testament Israel differs substantially from the obedience of New Testament saints, who have been freed from this works-arrangement through the death and resurrection of Christ.

The three editors of *The Law Is Not of Faith* (hereafter, *TLNF*), Bryan D. Estelle, J. V. Fesko, and David VanDrunen, are all OPC ministers and serve as professors of Westminster Seminary California (WSC). This book is targeting the ecclesiastical world of the Reformed church in general. However, a good case may be made that the book is uniquely relevant to the Orthodox Presbyterian Church (OPC), to which the editors and three other contributors belong (a total of six of the eleven participants). As was mentioned above, Meredith Kline (also an OPC minister) clearly stands behind the formulations in the book. His teaching may be identified as the primary source for the editors' own understanding of the doctrine of republication. However, the book also pays considerable attention to the theology of John Murray, one of the OPC's founding fathers. The editors have determined that he is particularly responsible for much of the resistance to this doctrine of republication in our denomination and beyond. They fear that this resistance may lead to the total loss of the doctrine in the Reformed churches.

In this book, we propose to set the context for the present debate in the church, as well as introduce the reader to some of our concerns about the republication doctrine. In part 1, we will seek to show that the *TLNF*-Klinean version of the doctrine of republication is the result of a modern-day debate concerning the doctrine of justification which began at Westminster Theological Seminary (Philadelphia) in the late 1970s. In our judgment, this debate ultimately resulted in a reactionary pendulum swing against

2. Westminster Confession of Faith (hereafter, WCF) 7.2; 19.1.

the teaching of Professor Norman Shepherd. Shepherd's teaching eventually deviated from historic Reformed covenant theology in that the doctrine of the covenant of works was compromised. This ultimately led to a deficient view of the doctrine of justification in which the imputation of the active obedience of Christ was explicitly repudiated. In response to Shepherd, Professor Meredith Kline sought to preserve the church's teaching on the covenant of works and justification through Christ's active obedience. However, Kline did this by making several of his own modifications to traditional Reformed theology, especially the doctrine of merit. In the end, we believe both sides have embraced and affirmed concepts that significantly differ from the confessional Reformed tradition. It has also become apparent that *TLNF* reflects and continues to promote the Klinean view of republication.

In part 2, we will seek to show how this pendulum swing resulted in a redefinition of the traditional concept of merit. This redefinition was first applied to the notion of Adamic merit in the original covenant of works. In the development of Kline's teaching, it also came to undergird and shape Israel's "typological merit" in the republished covenant of works under Moses. This reformulation of merit is further connected to the nature of the Mosaic covenant as it is separated into two levels in Kline's system. On the one hand, there is a grace level for the eternal salvation of the individual. On the other hand, there is a national, meritorious-works level for the retention of temporal earthly blessings. It is these ideas, which resulted from the pendulum swing, that the present writers believe undergird what is presented in *TLNF*.

In part 3, we will seek to show how the redefinition of merit and the division of the Mosaic covenant into two levels leads to an unstable theological paradigm. Not only do these new definitions fail to harmonize with those contained in the Westminster Standards, they create a "Republication Paradigm" which may lead to other systematic changes in our confessional theology. Ironically, the republication teaching, which was intended to preserve and protect the doctrine of justification, may (when consistently worked out) actually undercut this doctrine—the very doctrine by which the church stands or falls.

Finally, in our conclusion, we will rehearse our concerns in a summary fashion to support our conviction that the church needs to carefully evaluate this doctrinal formulation and consider its repercussions.

PART 1

Background to the Republication Paradigm

The introduction to *The Law Is Not of Faith* (*TLNF*) opens with the story of a presbytery exam. In this fictional story, a candidate for the ministry is being questioned regarding his views on the doctrine of republication. All the typical questions about this view are raised by the ministers and ruling elders. Rather than clearing up those concerns, the candidate's answers lead to confusion in the presbytery because his views are different from what they expect to hear and have heard before. What is the cause of the confusion? Is it: (1) historical or confessional ignorance on the part of the presbytery; or (2) a lack of precision and even reformulation of the Reformed tradition on the part of the candidate? The editors of *TLNF* would have us believe it is the former. In their opinion, the church's ignorance has called into question a view of the Mosaic covenant that has the highest Reformed pedigree. This fictional exam demonstrates that the editors believe the agitation in the church over republication stems from a fundamental misunderstanding of the doctrine, which then leads to its resistance or even outright rejection in Reformed churches. In this book, we will argue that the primary cause of confusion and agitation is the latter (2, above). Despite claims to the contrary, recent versions of

Part 1: Background to the Republication Paradigm

the republication doctrine (as reflected in the articles of *TLNF*) have redefined important theological concepts which are central to the historic Reformed system of doctrine. In our view, this has led to the creation of an unstable theological paradigm.

1

Introduction to *The Law Is Not of Faith*

THE BOOK'S PURPOSE: A PLEA FOR TOLERANCE OR A NEED FOR RECOVERY?

TLNF begins by issuing a plea for tolerance. According to the editors, the doctrine of republication ought to be recognized as being well within the bounds of confessional Reformed orthodoxy. But as one reads further, it becomes apparent that *TLNF* is arguing for much more than that. Rather than mere toleration, *TLNF* defends the idea that the doctrine of republication is part of the "warp and woof" of Scripture and historic Reformed thought.[1] Thus, the loss of the republication doctrine has the potential to lead (and in some cases, has already led) to a compromise of confessional Reformed theology.

The editors are convinced that the church is currently in a kind of republication "dark age." Due to various factors, this key component of Reformed covenant theology has been lost in the contemporary church.

1. *TLNF*, 6.

> Did such silence, dare we say historical ignorance, lead
> to a kind of unwitting torpor in the thinking of ministers,
> exegetes, and theologians in areas of theological inquiry
> such as the nature of the law, grace, typology, and merit?[2]

The task of *TLNF*, as the editors see it, is to help enlighten the
church and sound the alarm regarding the adverse effects of this
recent ignorance regarding republication. They view themselves as
calling for a return to the purer covenant theology of a brighter age,
in which the doctrine of republication was a "dominant concern
with so many Reformed luminaries in the past."[3] They intend to
remove the various historical, exegetical, and theological obstacles
to the doctrine, and in this way clear the way for the unequivocal
re-acceptance of this position in the church. The ultimate goal is
not simply for this doctrine of republication to be a permissible
minority view in the church, but to be embraced as something essential to its testimony to the Christ of the Scriptures.

Indeed, reading further in the book's introduction, one is
struck by the bold assertions regarding the editors' estimation of
this volume's importance. They believe that it is absolutely necessary for the church to embrace their theological formulation of
the Mosaic covenant. They assert that *TLNF* should receive a wide
reading because the recovery and promulgation of republication
is important (even essential?) for the vitality and well being of the
church. They press home their case with the following reasons.

> First, if ministers let the doctrine of republication die out
> and do not teach it faithfully, then they destroy a part of
> Old Testament typology that God gave for the edification
> of the church. Secondly, if there really is some principle
> of works operative in the Mosaic economy, and it is not
> just hypothetical but it is put there by God's design, then
> we dare not do injury to our own selves by ignoring what
> God has placed in his holy Word for our instruction.[4]

2. Ibid., 15.
3. Ibid.
4. Ibid., 18–19.

Note the claims being made about the doctrine of republication. To *ignore* and fail to teach it is *destructive* of *typology* and even dangerous, in that its neglect will lead to our own *injury*.

THE BOOK'S PASSION: PRESERVING THE DOCTRINE OF JUSTIFICATION

Why is this the case? The editors further explain that the republication doctrine is not only essential for a robust and healthy typology, but is "integrally connected" to the heart of the Protestant Reformation—justification by faith alone.

> In short, the doctrine of republication is integrally connected to the doctrine of justification. The Mosaic law was necessary to make manifest a works principle that Christ the Messiah would have to fulfil.[5]

In our judgment, this statement provides the key to understanding the zeal and passion with which the editors defend the republication doctrine. Note again what is being claimed: the idea of a works principle in the Mosaic covenant is a necessary teaching which is *integrally connected* to the doctrine of justification. The term "integral" refers to something that is essential and necessary to a thing's completeness—that which serves as a constituent or foundational part of something else. In connecting the two doctrines in this way, the editors are asserting that the republication doctrine is thus essential and necessary for the completeness of justification. They conclude this section of the introduction by reinforcing the significance of their view in no uncertain terms.

> Since the doctrine of republication highlights the need for a true son of Israel to accomplish this righteousness, and ultimately does make manifest the obedience of Christ as the fulfillment of that demand, a misunderstanding of the Mosaic economy and silence on the works principle embedded there will only leave us

5. Ibid., 19.

9

> necessarily impoverished in our faith. We will see in only
> a thin manner the work of our Savior.[6]

Here then is the heart of the book's reason for existence.
Failure to faithfully teach the doctrine of republication *not only*
leads to the destruction of a part of Old Testament typology, but
also to the compromise and erosion of the doctrine of justification.
Please note again what is inferred about those who do not hold
to the doctrine of republication as presented in *TLNF*. A failure
to teach the republication position "will only leave us necessarily
impoverished in our faith" and "we will see in only a thin manner the work of our Savior." It seems that one may fairly conclude
that even the Westminster Confession of Faith (among other Reformed confessions) would fall prey to these charges if it does not
teach the republication doctrine! The zeal to preserve and guard
the doctrine of justification is always to be commended. We see
this doctrine (with Luther) as the doctrine upon which the church
stands or falls. However, the editors of *TLNF* seem to imply that
the doctrine of republication (complete with a meritorious works
principle) is the doctrine upon which justification stands or falls.
Is this going too far?

The answer must be a resounding "Yes!" This book is our ef-
fort to address the challenges being posed by *TLNF* to those who
do not hold to the republication doctrine. But before we tackle the
theological issues, we must first have a better grasp of the place
of this volume in the history of the church, particularly the OPC.
Here in part 1, we will set forth one evaluation of that history.
Our assessment, in a nutshell, is as follows: *TLNF's* doctrine of republication represents a reactionary pendulum swing against the
views of Norman Shepherd and the Federal Vision (FV) theology.
Although advocates of the republication view properly recognize
many of the deviant formulations in the Shepherd/FV theology,
many of the alternatives they propose are also problematic, and
warrant careful evaluation.

6. Ibid.

Over against what we see as pendulum swings on both sides (albeit in opposite directions), we propose a renewed appreciation for the theological balance of the Westminster Standards, which serve as a *plumb line* for faithful scriptural teaching. In order to understand these dual pendulum swings, we must begin by assessing the place that John Murray's teaching occupies in the present debate.

2

TLNF and John Murray

IS MURRAY TO BLAME FOR OUR FORGETFULNESS?

As noted above, *TLNF* argues that "the doctrine of republication is integrally connected to the doctrine of justification," and that a failure to hold and teach the republication view will lead to injurious consequences. In the estimation of the editors, the republication teaching was an aspect of historic Reformed theology only recently lost by the contemporary church. How did we come to forget this important doctrine? According to *TLNF*, those of us in the OPC need look no further than our own John Murray, who taught at Westminster Theological Seminary (WTS) in Philadelphia (1930–1967).

According to the editors, Professor Murray, who "exercised a profound influence on generations of pastors and teachers"[1] is primarily responsible for turning the church against the republication doctrine.

1. *TLNF*, 15.

With such rhetoric, Murray released the clutch, and those who had studied under him or were influenced by his writings without appropriate reflection and criticism in these areas set in motion a chain of events that would produce deleterious injuries for confessional Reformed theology and beyond.[2]

What time period is in view? This is the time that coincides with the founding of the OPC in 1936 and the years that followed. His influence was primarily felt through the preaching and teaching of OPC ministers who were being trained under him at WTS and going out to serve in the newly formed denomination. Please note that the editors of *TLNF* are saying that in embracing Murray's theology, key founders of the OPC led the church down a treacherous theological path. In *TLNF*, they are advocating a new road—a safer road—one that is not fraught with such danger. Their path will not lead us to "see in only a thin manner the work of our Savior"; nor will it potentially (if not unavoidably) lead to the destruction of the doctrine of justification. In the eyes of the authors of *TLNF*, the OPC has been on a path to the compromise of confessional orthodoxy since its founding. Their task, as they see it, is to put the church back on the right path by exposing Murray's failure to do justice to the Reformed and biblical idea of republication. Put simply, the pre-Murray era was a kind of "golden age" for republication teaching. One of the primary purposes of *TLNF* is to help the OPC (and other Reformed churches) recover this "golden age" of theology and steer the church away from the influence of John Murray.

How do we know the old road inevitably leads from Murray to danger? The *TLNF* editors go on to say: "Norman Shepherd, professor of systematic theology at Westminster Theological Seminary from 1963 to 1982, is a case in point."[3] John Murray's theology was and continues to be dangerous to the church because Murray "released the clutch" down the road that inevitably leads to Norman Shepherd, and his company (Federal Vision, as well as

2. Ibid., 17.
3. Ibid.

the likes of Daniel Fuller). Among other things, Murray is charged with the following:

> Not only did he see the need for "recasting" covenant theology and especially the confessional and classical doctrine of the covenant of works, but he also eschewed the notion that the Sinaitic covenant was in some sense a "repetition of the so-called covenant of works."[4]

> Additionally, Murray was at least monocovenantal in the sense that he affirmed no other kind of covenant than a covenant of redemptive grace and, in doing so, he ironically blurred distinctions between the covenant of works and grace.[5]

Are these charges fair? Is it true that Murray's path is dangerous, and leads to Shepherd's theology? There is repeated mention being made of Murray's desire to "recast" covenant theology in a monocovenantal direction,[6] which is said to confuse works and grace in the covenant. The authors of *TLNF* are referring to the following statement made by Murray in his booklet, *The Covenant of Grace*.

> It appears to me that the covenant theology, notwithstanding the finesse of analysis with which it was worked out and the grandeur of its articulated systematization, needs recasting.[7]

The reasonable question to ask is, "What did Murray mean by this?" Is this statement to be interpreted as a bold rejection of the covenant theology of the Westminster Standards? We think not. This *single* statement from one published lecture has been taken

---

4. Ibid., 15–16.

5. Ibid., 16.

6. Monocovenantal is a word used to describe theology that affirms only one (mono) covenant in the Bible. This stands in contrast with the historic understanding, expressed in the Reformed creeds, that there are two (bi) covenants in the Bible, the covenant of works and the covenant of grace.

7. Murray, *Covenant of Grace*, 5.

out of its original context and emphasized as if Murray was advocating a significant break from the Reformed tradition.

WHAT DID MURRAY MEAN BY "RECASTING"?

So what did Professor Murray mean when he referred to the need for the "recasting" of covenant theology? In the context of *The Covenant of Grace*, immediately following the above quote, Murray explains how "covenant" has frequently been formulated in terms of a mutual agreement between two parties in the history of covenant theology. He then makes clear that his reference to "recasting" was specifically focused on this *one* particular aspect of the *definition* of "covenant":

> The question is simply whether the biblico-theological study will disclose that, in the usage of Scripture, covenant (*berith* in Hebrew and *diatheke* in Greek) may properly be interpreted in terms of a mutual pact or agreement.[8]

Thus, what Murray meant when he said that covenant theology "needs recasting" was specifically restricted to this point, and he was not alone in his thinking.[9] He believed a biblical covenant between God and man was better understood as a relationship that was initiated by God and sovereignly administered. This emphasis in Murray's teaching is now commonly accepted and taught.

8. Ibid., 8.

9. Murray notes: "There has been, however, a recognition on the part of more recent students of covenant theology that the idea of pact or compact or contract is not adequate or proper as the definition of *berith* and *diatheke* and admirable service has been rendered by such scholars in the analysis and formulation of the biblical concept. Cf. Geerhardus Vos . . . Herman Bavinck . . . G. Ch. Aalders . . . John Kelly . . . David Russell . . . Herman N. Ridderbos" (*Covenant of Grace*, 7).

WHAT DID MURRAY ACTUALLY TEACH?

What about the other statements made about Murray's covenant theology in *TLNF*? Was he "monocovenantal" in his covenant formulation? Did he advocate significant changes to the substance of covenant theology in the Reformed tradition, either implicitly or explicitly, as he is charged? Again, we believe that Murray is misrepresented on these points. What did Murray actually teach about the covenants, and how does his teaching measure up to the confessional standards of the church?

Murray did *not* seek to alter the substance of covenant theology, but did prefer to use different terminology. He chose to use the label *Adamic administration* for what is traditionally called the *covenant of works*. Murray would argue that Scripture nowhere designates God's relationship with Adam as being "covenantal." In his judgment, a biblical covenant applied only to the post-fall situation. This explains why he defined "covenant" in terms of a "sovereign administration of grace and promise."[10] He did not apply this definition to Adam's situation, to what is traditionally called the "covenant of works." For Murray, the term "covenant of works" might give the mistaken impression (especially when contrasted with the term "covenant of grace") that there were no elements of (non-redemptive) grace before the fall. Here we may think of the first section of chapter 7 of the Westminster Confession, which is foundational for the Reformed doctrine of the covenants. It speaks of God's *voluntary condescension*, which is manifested in a special act of providence,[11] by which he enters into covenant with Adam. For Murray, as well as many Reformed theologians throughout history, this condescension of God was gracious (in a non-redemptive sense). In other words, it was expressive of God's free, unmerited favor. It also should be noted that Murray did seem to allow the use of the term "covenant" to describe the relationship with Adam, though he preferred (for the reason just given) to use

---

10. Murray, *Covenant of Grace*, 16.

11. See Westminster Shorter Catechism (hereafter, WSC) 12.

the phrase "covenant of life," as found in the Westminster Shorter Catechism.[12]

What is important to underscore is that, while Murray preferred the use of different labels, he affirmed the *essential* parts or *substance* of the covenant of works and of the covenant of grace, as outlined in the Westminster Standards. In fact, his rejection of the term "covenant of works" to describe what he called "the Adamic administration" stemmed, in part, from his desire to preserve its unique character.[13] Since the term "covenant" was (according to Murray) a sovereign administration of grace and promise in a specifically *redemptive* context, such an idea would be inappropriate in Adam's thoroughly non-redemptive situation. Read in this light, Murray's preference to restrict the term "covenant" to the post-fall situation is actually indicative of his concern to preserve the non-redemptive "legal" character of Adam's original situation.[14]

PROFESSOR ROBERT STRIMPLE'S ASSESSMENT OF MURRAY

The present writers all sat under Professor Robert B. Strimple's teaching at WSC. Strimple helped establish the seminary in 1979–1980, served as its first president, and taught systematic theology for many years. Strimple's class notes, printed in his Doctrine of Christ syllabus, contain a helpful critique of Murray's understanding of covenant theology relative to the points mentioned above. Strimple was profoundly influenced as a student by Murray, and he always spoke with high respect for his former professor. Nevertheless, Strimple voices his disagreement with Murray regarding his desire to change the traditional terminology and to restrict the definition of covenant to the post-fall covenant of grace.

12. See Murray, *Collected Writings*, 4:261–62.

13. See Murray's discussion on this point, in which he states, "Whether or not the administration is designated covenant, the uniqueness and singularity must be recognized" (*Collected Writings*, 2:50).

14. See WCF 7.2 regarding Adam's perfect obedience as the condition of the covenant of works.

He [Murray] could say that a Biblical covenant is AL-WAYS a dispensation of GRACE to man because he refused to speak of the Adamic administration as a covenant, in spite of the fact that the Biblical revelation of that administration evidences the essential characteristics of a covenant, and indeed that administration is referred to as a covenant, I believe, in Hosea 6:7. I believe we have ample warrant to view the Adamic administration as a COVENANT, and I therefore cannot agree with Murray on this second point. (It might be thought that perhaps Mr. Murray could have defined a Biblical covenant as always a dispensation of grace to man even if he had been willing to view the original Adamic administration as a covenant, because of his willingness to speak of "the elements of grace entering that administration" (vol. 2, p. 49 [of Murray's *Collected Works*]). It was his insistence, however, that "Scripture always uses the term covenant . . . in reference to a provision that is redemptive or closely related (Noahic covenant, rbs) to redemptive design."

I might simply note in passing that here is another point on which I disagree with Professor Murray; i.e., in his willingness to speak of the "grace" involved in the Adamic administration. While it is certainly true that that administration evidenced God's goodness—the very fact that a promise of eternal life was held before Adam when no special reward was owing to man for obedience, perfect obedience being owed by the creature to his Creator in any case; and the fact that the promise spoke of an eternal life of confirmed holiness, a reward out of all proportion to the condition to be fulfilled—I believe that we do well to restrict the Biblical term, "grace," to specifically redemptive grace. And my fear is that to speak of "the elements of grace" in the Adamic administration may so play down the very real and tremendously important distinction between the covenant of works and the covenant of grace as to blur the distinctive character of each.[15]

---

15. Strimple, "Doctrine of Christ Syllabus," 54–55.

The present writers agree with Professor Strimple's assessment and critique of Murray on the above points. Despite these disagreements, it is important to emphasize that Murray did not reject any *essential* confessional component that makes the covenant of works ("Adamic administration") unique and distinctive from the covenant of grace. Thus, to say that Murray is a mono-covenantalist, who "ironically blurred the distinctions between the covenant of works and grace,"[16] is simply misleading, and in the end, inaccurate. Instead, it is factual to say that Murray *substantially* agrees with the classic Reformed formulations of the warp and woof of historic covenant theology. This becomes clear when we compare Murray's teaching with the church's creeds.

MURRAY AND THE PLUMB LINE OF THE WESTMINSTER STANDARDS

The Westminster Confession of Faith and Larger and Shorter Catechisms serve as the secondary standards for the OPC and several other Reformed denominations. They are a faithful summary of the teaching of Scripture. We will refer to these standards as a *plumb line* for the faith and life of the church. All teaching about the covenants is to be assessed in light of the creeds of a confessional church. Teachings constructed by John Murray, Norman Shepherd, and Meredith Kline and those who hold to republication doctrine, all need to be evaluated in light of, and measured against, the standard of this plumb line.

MURRAY AND THE COVENANT OF WORKS

How does Murray's view of the covenant of works / Adamic administration compare with the definition contained in the Westminster Confession? What are the essential parts of the covenant of works? These are clearly identified in WCF 7.2.

16. *TLNF*, 16.

> Wherein life was promised to Adam; and in him to his posterity, upon condition of perfect and personal obedience.

There can be no question that Murray affirms that life was promised to Adam, and in him, to his posterity. Murray affirms that the condition for receiving the promised reward was perfect and personal obedience.[17] The OPC's *Report on Justification* concurs.

> Murray, however, did affirm the necessity of Adam's perfect obedience and the promise of eschatological life if he did obey.[18]

This is also the judgment that Mark Jones makes in his review of *TLNF*.

> I recognize that some of the authors might feel uncomfortable with what they perceive to be "monocovenantal" tendencies in thinkers like Murray. For my own part, I fail to see how Murray can be described as a monocovenantalist. While he rejects the terminology of the covenant of works, he nevertheless affirms the substance of the doctrine. See "Adamic Administration" where he argues: "The condition was obedience" (http://www.the-highway.com/adamic-admin_Murray.html). That he "flattens" out the covenant of grace does not make him a monocovenantalist, though it may make him orthodox. See also Ch. 8 in Murray's *Principles of Conduct* (Grand Rapids: Eerdmans, 1957) titled "Law and Grace" (57ff).[19]

Thus, there should be no debate that Murray affirmed the *substance* of WCF 7.2. Although he preferred to call the arrangement with Adam an "administration" rather than a "covenant," he clearly did not "blur" the pre-fall and post-fall situations. In fact,

---

17. Murray writes, "So a period of obedience successfully completed by Adam would have secured eternal life for all represented by him"; and, "The condition was obedience . . . obedience unreserved and unswerving in all the extent of divine obligation" (*Collected Writings*, 2:49, 51).

18. OPC, *Report on Justification*, 7.

19. Jones, review of *TLNF*, 116n3.

he sought to guard the *substantial* differences between (what are traditionally termed) the covenants of works and grace.

MURRAY AND JUSTIFICATION

What about the doctrine of justification? Was Murray soft on justification? Does his theology necessarily lead down the road to Shepherd and the loss of the imputation of the active obedience of Christ that we find among the teachings of the proponents of Federal Vision? One only has to read Murray's outstanding volume *The Imputation of Adam's Sin* (not to mention other places) to know that he was among the greatest twentieth-century defenders and expositors of the doctrine of justification and the necessity of the imputation of the active obedience of Christ. His writings have been a great aid in helping many to better understand this essential doctrine, including the present writers.

Indeed, it is puzzling to read the kinds of concerns being expressed about Murray in *TLNF*. This is especially true in light of the additional testimony of two of the "fathers" of the OPC. Most OPC members are familiar with the story about the telegram sent by Professor J. Gresham Machen on his deathbed in North Dakota to Professor Murray: "I'm so thankful for active obedience of Christ. No hope without it." Meredith Kline notes this at the beginning of his article, "Covenant Theology Under Attack."[20] In the unedited version of the article, he seems perplexed as to why Murray would receive the telegram when, in his view, Murray undermines the doctrine of Christ's active obedience.

> Strangely, it was the one who received Machen's death-bed telegram who opened the door a considerable crack for the views inimical to the doctrine of the active obedience of Christ.[21]

Why did Machen choose to send those dying words about his hope in the imputation of Christ's active obedience to Murray?

20. Kline, "Covenant Theology."
21. Kline, "Covenant Theology" (unpublished version), para. 24.

Professor Cornelius Van Til, another founding father, helps answer this question. In a letter to Murray, who was ill and nearing the end of his days on earth, Van Til wrote:

> As I write I think of Dr Machen, lying on his death-bed in Bismarck, North Dakota, sending you a telegram: "How wonderful is the active obedience of Christ!" You had helped him see the significance of this aspect of his Saviour's work as he had never seen it before.[22]

It seems that Kline and the authors of *TLNF* share quite a different opinion of Murray than did Machen, Van Til, and Strimple. For *TLNF*, Murray's theology does (implicitly) "leave us necessarily impoverished in our faith" and seeing "only in a thin manner the work of our Savior."[23] For these founding fathers of the OPC, Murray helped them see the significance of Christ's work "as [they] had never seen it before!" It is clear, indeed, in light of the plumb line of the Confession, that the opinions expressed in *TLNF* are misleading and unwarranted. Despite our disagreement with Murray regarding certain terminology (as Professor Strimple pointed out), the *substance* of his covenant theology was confessional and is situated in the mainstream of the history of Reformed thought. Additionally, he was a great champion of the doctrine of the two-Adam scheme, as well as the all-important doctrines of justification by faith and the imputation of the active obedience of Christ. This explains why Murray and his writings have been so helpful and greatly appreciated within the OPC and beyond.

22. Murray, *Life of John Murray*, 202.
23. *TLNF*, 19.

3

Recasting Covenant Theology
(Part 1)

A Pendulum Swing—"Grace" before the Fall

SHEPHERD'S COVENANT THEOLOGY

Where do we go from here? We believe the evidence will show that the theological formulations of Norman Shepherd and Federal Vision, rather than lining up with the teaching of John Murray, resulted in a pendulum swing away from the plumb line of the Westminster Standards.

Norman Shepherd took Murray's place in 1963, teaching systematic theology at WTS in Philadelphia from 1963–1982. Robert Strimple also taught with Shepherd at WTS from 1969 until the spring of 1979. (Strimple left to establish Westminster Seminary California in the fall of 1979.) At WTS in Philadelphia, controversy arose over Shepherd's teaching on the covenants and the doctrine of justification. In 1982, he was dismissed from the seminary after seven years of controversy. He then transferred from the OPC to the Christian Reformed Church (CRC), pastored two

CRC congregations in the Midwest, and retired from the pastoral ministry in 1998.

What critique may be given of Norman Shepherd's views? This is difficult to answer since his views developed and changed over time. Nevertheless, we may identify three aspects of Shepherd's teaching and writings that show that he eventually deviated from the plumb line of the Westminster Standards.

1. Monocovenantalism

Shepherd denies the covenants of works/grace distinction. Unlike Murray, Shepherd deviated from the substance of chapter 7 of the Confession's teaching on the Covenants. Sections 2 and 3 of this chapter clearly make an *essential* or *substantial* distinction between the covenant of works and the covenant of grace. Shepherd rejected the teaching that the covenant with Adam was a covenant of works, preferring instead to speak of it as love covenant, more like a marriage, or the relationship between a father and son. He denied that any form of merit played a role in covenant relationships between God and man. In doing so, he rejected the *essential* distinction between the covenants of works and grace in the Westminster Standards. Unlike Murray, Shepherd came to embrace a truly monocovenantal position.[1]

2. Covenant Condition

Shepherd embraced what he refers to as the way of *covenant faithfulness* as the condition God required in every covenant administration. Again, how does Shepherd measure up to the plumb line of the Confession? WCF 7.2 states the condition of the covenant of works was *perfect and personal obedience* for Adam. WCF 7.3 specifies that the condition of the covenant of grace is *faith in the*

---

1. For a fuller treatment of Shepherd's view, see his work, *The Way of Righteousness*, and a pamphlet called "Law and Gospel in Covenantal Perspective" (a lecture presented on March 11, 2004, at a symposium entitled *Trust and Obey: A Symposium on Law and Gospel*, held in Warrenville, IL).

Mediator, Jesus Christ. Unlike Murray, Shepherd rejects the two covenants (not only in name but in substance) and, therefore, combines the conditions of these two covenants into a single condition for the single covenant that he espouses. That single condition which unites the administration of the covenant for Adam, Israel, Christ, and the New Testament believer, is *covenant faithfulness.* In his review of Norman Shepherd's book *The Call of Grace,* Cornel Venema (professor of doctrinal studies and president of Mid-America Reformed Seminary) writes:

> Shepherd treats the covenant relationship between God and his people *as largely identical at every point, including its administration before and after the fall into sin* . . . This flattening out or virtual identifying of the pre- and post-fall covenants has unavoidable and mischievous implications for our understanding of the way of salvation. For example, one implication of Shepherd's argument is that the way of salvation, whether for Adam or Christ or any believer, is always one and the same—the way of covenant-keeping faithfulness . . . Salvation is by grace through faith(fulness), before as well as after the fall. God's promise secures or guarantees the believer's covenant inheritance. However, that inheritance can only be received by way of the believer's covenant keeping.[2]

3. Justification

Shepherd eventually denied the imputation of the active obedience of Christ, which is foundational to the Reformed doctrine of justification. Shepherd not only rejected works in contrast to grace with Adam, but also the need for and reality of the imputed merits of Christ's active obedience for believers. The OPC's *Report on Justification* makes mention of this fact when it connects Shepherd's formulation and that found in the Federal Vision movement.

> The imputation of the active obedience of Christ to us for our justification is denied, however, by teaching

2. Venema, review of *Call of Grace,* 244, emphasis in original.

associated with or influencing the FV. Shepherd, for example, teaches that only the passive obedience of Christ is in view and is imputed in justification, and that the active obedience of Christ is not imputed to us for our justification.[3]

What is the concern? As the authors of *TLNF* have repeatedly indicated, and the OPC's *Report on Justification* has stated, the concern is to preserve the doctrine of justification by faith. The answer to Westminster Shorter Catechism Q. 33 states this doctrine clearly and concisely.

> Justification is an act of God's free grace, wherein he pardoneth all our sins, and accepteth us as righteous in his sight, only for the righteousness of Christ imputed to us, and received by faith alone.

The imputation of the full obedience of Christ (both active and passive) is the ground of the believer's righteous standing before God. Professor Shepherd went too far by truly *recasting* covenant theology into a different mold, mixing and confusing grace and works in the covenant. We can sincerely give thanks for the role that some of the authors of *TLNF* played in helping our denomination clarify the matter in the *Report on Justification*.

By way of summary, in place of the essential and substantial distinction between the covenants of works and grace (including their respective covenant conditions), Shepherd spoke of the call to covenant faithfulness on the part of Adam, Christ, and the believer alike throughout a single covenant of grace. Furthermore, the uniqueness of the federal headships of Adam and Christ is lost as the line which distinguishes grace from works is blotted out. As an end result, Shepherd's theology makes fallen human covenant keeping the way of receiving the inheritance of eternal life. In our opinion, these distinctive points in Shepherd's theology, as well as his denial of the imputation of the active obedience of Christ in justification, places him beyond the pale of the Westminster Standards, as well as other Reformed creeds and confessions.

3. OPC, *Report on Justification*, 71.

SHEPHERD AND MURRAY ESSENTIALLY DIFFER

In light of the above treatment of the teachings of Professors Murray and Shepherd, as they are measured against the plumb line of the Westminster Confession, it is baffling how the editors of *TLNF* see Shepherd not only as the successor to Murray's chair in Systematic Theology at Westminster, but as the theological heir and descendant of Murray's theology of the covenants. As we have demonstrated, Shepherd differed from Murray on *two* central questions in the present debate. First, Shepherd disagreed with Murray on restricting the term "covenant" to the post-fall situation. Shepherd regularly refers to God's pre-fall arrangement with Adam as being a "covenant." Second, he explicitly departed from Murray's insistence that Adam was under obligation to perform perfect, personal obedience to the commandments as the legal basis of his attainment of the reward of life.

In spite of this, the authors of *TLNF* believe that the OPC needs the one and true remedy for ridding the denomination of the bad fruits of *Shepherd-ism* (in all its varieties), by laying the proverbial axe to its root in *Murray-ism*. That axe, as we have shown, is the doctrine of republication, following Meredith G. Kline. Yet in the next chapter, it will become clear how the republication viewpoint is itself a reactionary theological pendulum swing away from the plumb line of the Confession.

4

Recasting Covenant Theology (Part 2)

A Reactionary Pendulum Swing—Works/ Merit in the Mosaic Covenant

KLINE AND THE SHEPHERD DEBATE

During the course of the seven years of faculty debate over the views of Norman Shepherd, Meredith Kline served as professor at Gordon-Conwell Theological Seminary but was still teaching part-time at WTS in Philadelphia. There he became involved with the Shepherd debate and made it well known that he was vigorously opposed to Shepherd's views. This period of controversy would leave a lasting impact on Kline's theology and writing. One need look no further than his *Kingdom Prologue*, which was a primary text for many of his classroom lectures. In it, he devotes an entire section to laying the basis for the doctrine of republication, which is explicitly written to combat Norman Shepherd's covenant paradigm. It also serves to summarize several other writings by Kline devoted to this same topic.

> The following discussion of this radical departure from
> the classic law-gospel contrast reflects my studies "Of
> Works and Grace," *Presbyterion* 9 (1983) 85–92 and
> "Covenant Theology Under Attack," *New Horizons* 15/2
> (1994) 3–5, critiques of the teachings of the Daniel P.
> Fuller-John Piper-Norman Shepherd school.[1]

This statement helps demonstrate that Kline's concerns over Shepherd's theology were front and center in his writings and in the formulation of his own views on the Mosaic covenant.

KLINE'S 1994 OPC NEW HORIZONS ARTICLE

During his years in the pastoral ministry after his dismissal from Westminster (from 1982 until 1992), Professor Shepherd did not publish his views on covenant theology. In 1992, he published an article, to which Professor Kline eventually responded.[2] That response appeared in the February 1994 edition of the OPC's magazine, *New Horizons*, with the title "Covenant Theology Under Attack." Reportedly, the editor at that time of *New Horizons* asked Kline to tone down the tenor of the article by removing and altering certain portions which referred to John Murray and Norman Shepherd.[3]

The article is Kline's defense of the imputation of Christ's active obedience from the theological attacks on Reformed covenant theology from Daniel Fuller and Norman Shepherd. One of the paragraphs omitted in the *New Horizons* version shows that the purpose of the article was to combat Norman Shepherd as much as Daniel Fuller.

> The door left ajar by Murray was thrown wide open
> to Fuller's theology by Murray's successor . . . Norman

1. Kline, *Kingdom Prologue*, 108.

2. Shepherd, "Need to Persevere (II)," 20–21.

3. This statement is based on the present authors' recollection from seminary class with Prof. Kline, as well as the remark made by Lee Irons as he introduces the original version of the article on his website: "What follows is the unexpurgated text."

Shepherd rightly rejected Murray's notion of a state of nature. (Such a pre-covenant situation never existed; the world was created a covenantal order from the outset.) However, this meant that for Shepherd, who adopted Murray's equation of covenant and "grace," there was no place at all left for a covenant of works or meritorious human obedience or simple justice. Though the ensuing controversy over Shepherd's views led to his departure, his teaching was not officially renounced by ecclesiastical or seminary arms of our movement, and key elements of the Fuller-Shepherd theology continue to be advocated among us.[4]

Two of the present writers were in Professor Kline's seminary class at WSC during the time in which this article was published. We remember how Professor Kline distributed the unedited, unpublished version of this article to his students. He then incorporated it into his classroom lectures by carefully reading through it, and providing further explanation along the way. In this version of the article, John Murray is explicitly connected to the errant theology of Daniel Fuller and Norman Shepherd. Professor Kline is remembered as stating very clearly that the class needed to read the full text because the doctrine of justification was at stake. As Kline stated in his article, he believed the Murray-Shepherd theology constituted a "subtle surrender to Rome." He made clear his conviction that Fuller's theology "undermines the Gospel of grace," and that it found its way into the OPC through the work of John Murray.

The door left ajar by Murray was thrown wide open to Fuller's theology by Murray's successor . . . Norman Shepherd[5]

Kline felt it was his duty to warn the church about the Murray-Shepherd-Fuller theology, which constituted an "encroachment of this radical renunciation of the Reformation, this subtle surrender to Rome."[6]

4. Kline, "Covenant Theology" (unpublished version), para. 26.
5. Ibid.
6. Ibid., para 27.

After his retirement, Professor Shepherd continued to write books and to give lectures. As was noted earlier, Shepherd has since published his views stating his rejection of both the doctrines of the covenant of works and the imputation of Christ's active obedience. In recent years, he has supported those who belong to the Federal Vision school through writing and lecturing.

To the present writers, it appears evident that Kline's criticisms of Murray and Shepherd are now being echoed and expanded by the editors of *TLNF* in the book's introduction. We remind the reader of what was quoted earlier.

> With such rhetoric, Murray released the clutch, and those who had studied under him or were influenced by his writings without appropriate reflection and criticism in these areas set in motion a chain of events that would produce deleterious injuries for confessional Reformed theology and beyond. Norman Shepherd, professor of systematic theology at Westminster Theological Seminary from 1963 to 1982, is a case in point.[7]

The parallels between Kline's 1994 article and the introduction to *TLNF* are striking, to say the least. Both tie the orthodox doctrine of justification by faith alone in some degree to a proper understanding of the Mosaic covenant, and both see the theology of John Murray as the chief cause of the aberrant teachings of Norman Shepherd and FV.

KLINE'S REACTIONARY THEOLOGY

As noted above, Kline and the authors of *TLNF* are correct to point to dangerous imbalances in the theology of Norman Shepherd and FV. But is it possible that even as Shepherd and FV represented a pendulum swing away from the Reformed creeds in one direction, Kline's reaction to it might constitute a swing in another? We may identify three components of Kline's teaching and writings intended to counteract the teaching of Shepherd and FV. In our

7. *TLNF*, 17.

view, these components do swing wide of the plumb line of the Westminster Standards.

1. Disagreement with Voluntary Condescension

In light of these controversies, Kline spoke of redefining the concept of grace to preserve the meritorious character of the covenant of works. Instead of the traditional Augustinian definition of grace as "unmerited favor," Kline proposed viewing grace more strictly as "demerited favor" (i.e., favor granted after man's fall in spite of demerit). He also questioned the Westminster Confession of Faith 7.1, which speaks of God's *voluntary condescension* to make a covenant with Adam. (He told faculty members, including Robert Strimple in a private conversation, that he took a personal exception to that particular wording of WCF 7.1.[8]) Since Murray and Shepherd spoke of gracious elements in God's relationship with man before the fall, Kline did not want to use vocabulary like God's *goodness, kindness,* or even *condescension* in entering into the covenant of works with Adam. Kline finally settled on speaking about God's *benevolence,* but not in the context of the doctrine of God's voluntary condescension (as outlined in WCF 7.1). Instead of referring to the necessity of God's condescension in establishing the covenant with its reward of eternal life, he sees the bestowal of the reward of the covenant as "an aspect of God's creational love." He sought to guard the attainment of the reward as "a matter of works" in distinction from grace.[9] As we will explore later in part 2, this is the result of the conflation of creation and covenant in Kline's system, which leads to the squeezing out of God's voluntary condescension, and a recasting of the covenantal formulation of the Westminster Standards.

8. Strimple, "Westminster Confession of Faith," 8.
9. Kline, *Kingdom Prologue,* 112.

2. Israel as a Corporate Typological Adam with a Merit-Based Probation

As Kline reacted to Shepherd's theology, he sought to demonstrate that the works principle was foundational to all of the divine covenants, and therefore, shut the door once and for all "to the sweeping denial of the operation of the works principle anywhere in the divine government."[10] One of the ways to do this is by comparing the two Adams, which is typical and necessary in Reformed covenant theology. If Christ's mission is to prevail where the first Adam failed, then "Adam, like Christ, must have been placed under a covenant of works."[11] In the standard Reformed view of Romans 5, we understand that Paul draws a comparison between the obedience of the two Adams as the respective covenant heads of the covenant of works and covenant of grace: "Therefore, as one trespass led to condemnation for all men, so one act of righteousness leads to justification and life for all men" (Rom 5:18).

But Kline does not stop with the comparison between the two Adams. He goes on to make Israel something of another *Adam figure* that he believes will fortify the two-Adam doctrine.

> Likewise, the identification of God's old covenant with Israel as one of works points to the works nature of the creational covenant. Here we can only state a conclusion that the study of biblical evidence would substantiate, but the significant point is that the old covenant with Israel, though it was something more, was also a re-enactment (with necessary adjustments) of mankind's probation—and fall. It was as the true Israel, born under the law, that Christ was the second Adam. This means that the covenant with the first Adam, like the typological Israelite re-enactment of it, would have been a covenant of law in the sense of works, the antithesis of the grace-promise-faith principle.[12]

10. Ibid., 108.
11. Ibid., 110.
12. Ibid.

Professor Kline taught that because the covenant with Israel provides the context for a historical reenactment of the probation of the first Adam, it also republishes the covenant of works. The works principle in the Mosaic covenant would therefore provide additional evidence against Shepherd that Adam was in a covenant governed by the works principle. In other words, if it can be shown that Old Testament Israel was under a national works principle, then it would be impossible to deny that Adam was under a works principle. The Mosaic covenant is designed to show that corporate Israel's relationship to God is a reenactment of Adam's probation and fall. This retrospective reasoning going from Israel's situation back to Adam's would demonstrate that "there can be no a priori objection to the standard view of the original Edenic order as a covenant of works."[13] This also means, however, that the Mosaic covenant's *essential* nature can no longer be characterized as a covenant of grace in Kline's formulation (contrary to WCF 7.3). Instead, it corresponds to the nature of the Adamic covenant. In Kline's words again, both the Adamic as well as the old covenant with Israel "would have been a covenant of law in the sense of works, the antithesis of the grace-promise-faith principle."[14] Thus, Kline taught that Israel was placed under a situation analogous to that of Adam, in which they were required to "maintain the necessary meritorious obedience."[15]

3. Israel's Meritorious Works as Typological of Christ's Obedience

Since Kline was seeking to show the importance of the republication view, in contrast to Shepherd's covenant formulation, he continued to draw a line of continuity from the obedience of Adam through Israel, to Christ. In this way, Israel's probation was not only a "reenactment" of Adam's, but also served as a type of the

13. Ibid.
14. Ibid.
15. Ibid., 109.

obedience of Christ. In Kline's system, the works principle operating in Israel under Moses thus illustrates and anticipates the necessity of the imputation of Christ's meritorious active obedience. For Kline, the works arrangement under which Christ is placed as Mediator only makes sense in connection with Israel's works arrangement. This point is affirmed and explained in the following way.

> It was therefore expedient, if not necessary, that Christ appear within a covenant order which, like the covenant with the first Adam, was governed by the works principle (see Gal 4:4). The typal kingdom of the old covenant was precisely that. Within the limitations of the fallen world and with modifications peculiar to the redemptive process, the old theocratic kingdom was a reproduction of the original covenantal order. Israel as the theocratic nation was mankind stationed once again in a paradise-sanctuary, under probation in a covenant of works. In the context of that situation, the Incarnation event was legible; apart from it the meaning of the appearing and ministry of the Son of Man would hardly have been perspicuous.[16]

> Thus, in addition to calling attention to the probationary aspect of Jesus' mission, the works principle that governed the Israelite kingdom acted as a schoolmaster for Israel, convicting of sin and total inability to satisfy the Lord's righteous demands and thereby driving the sinner to the grace of God offered in the underlying gospel promises of the Abrahamic Covenant.[17]

In this way, by looking forward to Christ and backwards to Adam, Kline underscored the continuity of the works principle in redemptive history. It runs not only from Adam to Christ, but also through corporate Israel in between. We may thus modify the familiar slogan about federal headship in this way: "Where Adam *and Israel* failed, Christ prevailed." In effect, there are now three

16. Ibid., 352.
17. Ibid., 353.

Adams in redemptive history, with Israel's meritorious works arrangement now functioning along with the first Adam's, as precursors to the meritorious work of Christ. Kline thus taught that the works principle in Israel served to show the need for the active obedience of Christ to merit the reward of life. Whereas Israel once sought to merit its retention of the typological reward—temporal life in the land—now Christ has come to merit eschatological life.

In sum, this distinctive element of Kline's Republication Paradigm is thus viewed as undergirding the doctrine of justification against the teaching of Shepherd and Federal Vision. It does this by showing that Israel serves as a type of Christ, as she both reenacts Adam's history and preenacts the merit-paradigm under which Christ is placed. Kline seeks to show unequivocally that the need for the imputation of the active obedience of Christ is anticipated in the Mosaic covenant in the *typological* and *pedagogical* works principle in the life of the nation of Israel (see following diagram).

Adam	<	Israel	>	Christ
Obedience		Typological Obedience		Active Obedience

According to Kline's republication teaching, the failure to view the Mosaic covenant as a merit-based probation has serious consequences. For Kline, the works principle in Israel becomes a key plank for the doctrines of the covenant of works and Christ's active obedience. Since Kline integrally links the Adamic and Mosaic covenants by way of a meritorious works principle, a modification of the latter would (in his system) lead to a necessary modification of the former. Kline is thus seeking to guard against Shepherd's formulation of a gracious covenant with Adam. This explains (in part) the zeal with which Kline and other proponents have promulgated and defended the doctrine of republication. It is just as *TLNF* put it: "In short, the doctrine of republication is integrally connected to the doctrine of justification."[18]

18. *TLNF*, 19.

KLINE IS THE SOURCE OF THE REPUBLICATION
VIEW IN TLNF

In spite of the book's claims to the contrary, we believe (with several reviewers of *TLNF*) that the Republication Paradigm was not the predominant view in the history of Reformed covenant theology. There are certainly those in the Reformed tradition who speak of the Mosaic covenant as reflecting aspects of the original covenant of works with Adam. But even these are quite different from the view proposed by Kline, which isolates the works element to the temporal arena and describes Israel's obedience as possessing a "meritorious" character. Although we acknowledge that certain points of similarity between the covenant of works and the Mosaic covenant can be found in previous writers, none of them argue a works-merit formula for Israel as a "corporate Adam," as Kline and his disciples propose.

Instead, in our view, the evidence shows that Meredith Kline is the architect of the contemporary Republication Paradigm described above. Kline was responding to a modern theological debate and discussion about the covenants, and his views are now being advocated by the authors of *TLNF* and other adherents of the republication doctrine. The present writers agree with the point Cornel Venema makes in his review.

> First, the stimulus and source for this understanding of the typology of the Mosaic covenant is undoubtedly the biblical-theological formulations of Meredith Kline. In the writings of Reformed theologians in what I have termed the "formative" period of the formulation of covenant theology, the language of a "works principle" in the Mosaic economy is not found. However, this language is frequently employed by Meredith Kline in his biblical theology of the covenants of works and of grace, and it is evident that Kline's formulations lie behind those of several of the authors of *The Law Is Not of Faith*. The idea that the covenant of works was republished "in some

sense" is a significant part of Kline's understanding of the distinctive nature of the Mosaic economy.[19]

Thus, it is our belief that in the republication teaching presented in *TLNF*, we see the evidence of a pendulum swing in reaction to Norman Shepherd's modern formulations of covenant theology.[20]

THE FAITHFUL PLUMB LINE OF THE WESTMINSTER CONFESSION OF FAITH

On the one hand, Shepherd's teaching led to a pendulum swing away from the Westminster Standards by rejecting the covenant of works. In its place, he recast the covenant of grace as a mono-covenantal enshrinement of the gracious condition of covenant faithfulness from creation to consummation. This condition was imposed upon all alike, from Adam and his descendants, to Christ and all who are united to him by faith. This has led to serious doctrinal errors, especially regarding justification. We are grateful for how the authors of *TLNF* joined many others in the church in sorting out a number of these errors.

On the other hand, the Republication Paradigm of Kline and the authors of *TLNF* has led to a pendulum swing away from the Westminster Standards in the opposite direction. This has occurred by bringing meritorious human works into the covenant of grace after the fall (i.e., in the Mosaic covenant). It is laudable that the proponents of the doctrine of republication passionately reject the mixture of faith and works in the covenant with Adam against Shepherd. Nevertheless, it is of equal concern that a similar mixture of individual faith and national works are brought into the covenant with Moses after the fall (see following diagram).

19. Venema, review of *TLNF*, 89.

20. Additionally, the recent work of James T. Dennison Jr. (which has resulted in the publication of *Reformed Confessions of the 16th and 17th Centuries in English Translation*, vols. 1–4) demonstrates that the Republication Paradigm of a typological works-merit covenant with Israel as a "corporate Adam" in the Mosaic era, is not found in any of the more than 125 Reformed confessions of the 16th and 17th centuries.

Adam	>	Israel	>	Christ
Perfect Obedience		Imperfect National Obedience		Perfect Obedience

What is more, these (imperfect) works after the fall are said to be operating within a paradigm where a group of fallen sinners can merit or extract a blessing from God. In Kline's writings, meritorious works become possible for other post-fall Old Testament figures prior to the Mosaic covenant (as we will see in part 2). How can this be? We believe the concept of merit that lies behind the Klinean republication teaching raises serious doctrinal concerns. When evaluated against the measuring line of our Confession and other Reformed creeds, additional questions and concerns about the republication view emerge. We will address these concerns in the remainder of this book.

The result of the controversy surrounding the Shepherd-FV theology was the establishment of an OPC study committee on justification. Their report has helped the church clarify these issues in light of Scripture and the system of doctrine contained in the Westminster Standards. We believe the republication doctrine similarly leads to imprecise theological formulations, as well as the redefinition of established Reformed concepts (as we will consider in part 3). This, in turn, leads to confusion. It is our contention that the church needs to give this contemporary republication teaching careful attention.

CONCLUSION OF PART 1

We need not fall prey to the confusion caused by the formulations of Shepherd and FV on the one side, nor those of Kline and the Republication Paradigm on the other. The Westminster Standards (and other Reformed creeds) embody the *consensus* formulations of historic Reformed theology. This plumb line has served as a faithful standard for faith and life for hundreds of years. More importantly, our church embraces the Westminster Standards as containing the system of doctrine taught in the holy Scriptures.

Indeed, we may be assured that our confidence in our Reformed creeds is well placed. They are proven guides and reliable signposts in navigating a biblically sound course among many potential deviations.

PART 2

Redefining Merit
The Klinean Paradigm Shift

In part 1, we spoke of a "Republication Paradigm" that differs in important respects from the Westminster Confession of Faith. We argued that these differences were the result of a pendulum swing against the paradigm of Norman Shepherd. In part 2, we will seek to show how this pendulum swing resulted in a redefinition of the traditional concept of merit. This redefinition was first applied to the notion of Adamic merit in the original covenant of works. In the development of Kline's teaching, it also came to undergird and shape Israel's "typological merit" in the republication of the covenant of works under Moses.

Our purpose in this section is to demonstrate that the Republication Paradigm and the Westminster Confession of Faith represent two different conceptions of "merit." One of the most significant differences between the two positions is the way in which the Republication Paradigm affirms merit for Old Testament figures after the fall. Clear examples of this can be found in the writings of Professor Kline and other contemporary authors (see below and appendices). The difference between this view and the traditional position cannot be more striking. The traditional view rejects any possibility for merit on the part of sinful man, in any sense, after the fall. The Republication Paradigm affirms that a type of merit is possible on the part of fallen man.

What is at the root of these differences between historic Reformed theology (as expressed in the Confession) and the contemporary republication formulation? The following four divisions will answer this question.

- Chapter 5: The term "merit" is being used in two different ways.

- Chapters 6: The historic definition of merit is part and parcel of the classic Augustinian-Reformation theology of the Westminster Confession.

- Chapter 7: The Republication Paradigm is a system that has *redefined* merit in a particular way, in contrast to—and over against—the Confession's earlier definition of merit.

- Chapter 8: The Republication Paradigm's *reformulation* of merit—following Meredith G. Kline—is connected to a novel view of the Mosaic covenant. Kline separated this covenant into two levels in his system. On the one hand, there was the "grace level" for the eternal salvation of the individual. On the other hand, there was a "national, meritorious-works level" for the retention of temporal earthly blessings

In these four chapters, we will explore the differences between merit in historic Reformed theology and its redefinition in the republication view. Further, it is our belief that this redefinition of merit is not an isolated modification that leaves the broader Reformed system of doctrine unaffected. Instead, this new conception of merit has paradigmatic implications that significantly modify other key doctrines. These will be taken up in part 3.

5

Two Different Uses of Merit

THE CONFESSIONAL PARADIGM HOLDS TO AN
AUGUSTINIAN DEFINITION OF MERIT

In traditional Reformed theology, merit has strictly and properly been defined as any "work to which a reward is due from justice on account of its intrinsic value and worth."[1] Merit, properly speaking, requires two essential things: (1) moral perfection; and (2) ontological equality. This historic Reformed view of merit is reflected in our Confession of Faith, and is rooted in its commitment to Augustinianism.

Augustine, in his debates with Pelagius and Pelagianism (AD 411/12–430), argued that human merits became impossible after Adam's fall into sin. This idea was based upon Scripture and lies at the heart of the doctrine of total depravity or total inability. Augustine argued that fallen humanity was incapable of earning any blessing or favor from God.

> Here let human merits, which have perished through Adam, keep silence, and let that grace of God reign

1. Turretin, *Institutes*, 2:710.

which reigns through Jesus Christ our Lord, the only Son of God.[2]

Augustine's debates with Pelagius revolved around man's ability to merit something from God after the fall. Augustine famously said, "Lord give what thou commandest, and command what thou wilt."[3] In other words, "Command what you will, O Lord, and give what you command." Augustine acknowledges that sinful man is unable to render the obedience that was required of Adam before the fall. It is no longer possible for a sinner to render personal, perfect, and perpetual obedience to God. Therefore, it is not possible for sinful man to merit any blessing from God, or claim that God was in his debt. God must graciously grant the ability to man to perform obedient service to the Lord ("Give what you command"). Augustine appealed to Scripture for support: "What do you have that you did not receive? If then you received it, why do you boast as if you did not receive it?" (1 Cor 4:7); and "who has given a gift to him that he might be repaid?" (Rom 11:35). The mere presence of redemptive grace eliminates the notion of human merit. The *Kerux* review of *TLNF* is helpful in understanding Augustine's primary concern.

> What emerges from Augustine's battle with Pelagius and the Pelagians is a ringing biblical definition of God's grace. Grace is a free, unmerited gift of God. It is free, that is, sovereignly dispensed. It is unmerited, that is no recipient is worthy of it nor can they perform any act deserving of it; it is a gift—what do you have that you have not received as a gift. Its source is God alone, no other. That Augustinian biblical notion of grace is the very antithesis of merit.[4]

Thus, Augustine persistently and comprehensively argued against even the possibility of merit on the part of man after the fall.

---

2. Augustine, *On the Predestination of the Saints*, 15.31, 5:513.

3. Augustine, *Confessions*, 10.29.40.

4. Dennison et al, review of *TLNF*, 18.

One example of the way this view of merit comprehensively affects our understanding of sinful man's position before God is found in the Larger Catechism.

> In the fourth petition, (which is, *Give us this day our daily bread*), [we acknowledge], that in Adam, and by our own sin, we have forfeited our right to all the outward blessings of this life, and deserve to be wholly deprived of them by God, and to have them cursed to us in the use of them; and that neither they of themselves are able to sustain us, nor we to merit, or by our own industry to procure them.[5]

The Catechism shows how the fourth petition of the Lord's Prayer reflects an Augustinian paradigm: "In Adam, and by our own sin, we have forfeited our right to all the outward blessings of this life." Fallen man is therefore unable "to merit, or by our own industry to procure" any kind of blessing, whether it be spiritual and eternal or temporal and material.[6]

---

5. Westminster Larger Catechism (hereafter, WLC) 193.

6. Note Calvin's Augustinian convictions (predating the Westminster Shorter Catechism) regarding Canaan and merit in a sermon on Deut 9:

> Now Moses comes to the second matter which we have touched, which ought to be well marked: namely, that when God has helped and succored us and done more for us than we looked for, or than our wit could conceive, we must yield him his deserved glory; so as we are not besotted with pride and overweening to challenge that to ourselves which belongs only unto God—let us beware of such unthankfulness. Again, let us not imagine that God serves his turn by us in respect of any worthiness of ours, but let us understand that his choosing of us is only in respect of his own good will. We shall not find any deserving at all in ourselves in this behalf, but it is of his free mercy only which he will have us to magnify above all things.
>
> True it is, that Moses speaks here of the land of Canaan. But if men cannot deserve [*meriter*, "merit" French text] anything [*ne . . . rien*, "nothing" French text] in this world in respect of transitory things, how shall they deserve [*meriteront-ils*, "they merit" French text] everlasting life? If I cannot win a little piece of ground, how shall I win a whole realm? So then, let us mark that of the things that are said here, we must gather a general doctrine

Only two figures in biblical history are able *in any sense* to merit or earn favor with God: Adam in his pre-fall state, and the Lord Jesus Christ. Only these two figures are capable of performing a work that is truly perfect, thus satisfying the demands of God's justice (an essential condition of a meritorious work before God). God's justice demands that our works be perfect. Since all of fallen man's works are imperfect, he can never at any time merit *any kind* of blessing from God (either temporal or eternal).

THE KLINEAN REPUBLICATION PARADIGM BRINGS MERIT BACK AFTER THE FALL

When we come to the Republication Paradigm, merit is being defined and used differently than in the Westminster Standards. In this paradigm, one might legitimately question how WLC 193 could apply to Old Testament believers under the Mosaic covenant. There the Catechism teaches that we cannot "merit, or by our own industry . . . procure" any of "the outward blessings of this life." However, proponents of the republication view have clearly and unequivocally taught that certain Old Testament figures did merit some outward blessings of this life in the promised land.

Some of the clearest examples of post-fall merit within the Republication Paradigm are found in the writings of Meredith G. Kline. Kline shows the breadth of the scope of his view of post-fall merit—a view that goes beyond what is explicitly stated within the

---

which is, that if the children of Israel were put in possession of the land that had been promised them, not for their own righteousness sake, but through God's free goodness, it is much more reason that when we speak of the heavenly life and of the inheritance of the heavenly glory, we should not dream upon any power of our own, but acknowledge that God has uttered his righteousness and showed his goodness in his vouchsafing to choose us (John Calvin, "The Lxii Sermon of Iohn Calvin" [on Deut 9:1–6], in *Sermons of M. Iohn Calvin vpon the Fifth Booke of Moses Called Deuteronomie*, 375–76; slight modernizing changes in spelling and punctuation have been made and insertions from the French version inserted for clarity).

pages of *TLNF* (although elsewhere some of the authors endorse his position). He speaks not only of meritorious works on the part of the nation of Israel under the Mosaic covenant, but also on the part of the pre-Mosaic figures of Noah and Abraham, who serve (by these works) as types of the Christ who was to come. Regarding Noah:

> In the case of some of these grantees, including Noah, their righteous acts were the grounds for bestowing kingdom benefits on others closely related to them . . . just as in the case of Christ.[7]

Regarding Abraham:

> Abraham, the grantee of the covenant promise. His exemplary obedience was invested by the Lord with typological significance as the meritorious ground for his descendants' inheritance of the promised land.[8]

Regarding Israel under Moses:

> The old covenant was law, the opposite of grace-faith, and in the postlapsarian world that meant it would turn out to be an administration of condemnation as a consequence of sinful Israel's failure to maintain the necessary meritorious obedience.[9]

Bryan Estelle serves as an example of a *TLNF* author who follows Kline in his understanding of post-fall merit.

> Although the substance of the covenant of grace is the same in both testaments, in the old covenant there was the need for compliance so that this would be the meritorious grounds for Israel's continuance in the land, the typological kingdom.[10]

---

7. Kline, *God, Heaven and Har Magedon*, 79.
8. Ibid., 127–28.
9. Kline, *Kingdom Prologue*, 109.
10. Estelle, "Leviticus 18:5," 136.

Estelle has also endorsed Kline's interpretation of Noah's obedience which we cited above.[11] Michael Horton, another contributor to *TLNF* has also embraced Kline's interpretation of Abraham's obedience.[12] Dennis Johnson (a colleague of the editors at WSC) has also endorsed this view.[13]

How is it possible for these theologians—all professing Augustinian Calvinists—to affirm the possibility of human merit after the fall? The key to understanding this element of their view of the Mosaic covenant is to recognize that these affirmations imply a *redefinition of the traditional concept of merit.* Put simply, the traditional view required that a work be perfect in order to merit before God. In the redefined view underlying the republication position, perfection is no longer absolutely necessary.

In summary, it is the present authors' contention that the Westminster Standards and the republication view embody two different conceptions of merit. The latter allows fallen humanity to perform meritorious works, albeit in the temporal realm. What accounts for this significant variation between these two paradigms? How did we get from Augustine's view or definition of merit to the republication doctrine, which allows for meritorious acts of obedience to be performed by Noah, Abraham, or Israel? We will explore the answers to these questions in the next three chapters.

---

11. Estelle, "Noah: A Righteous Man?," 27.

12. Horton, *God of Promise*, 44–45.

13. Johnson, *Him We Proclaim*, 298–99. To read relevant portions of the examples referenced here, see appendix 1.

6

Two Different Definitions of Merit (Part 1)

The Augustinian-Reformation Paradigm

THE AUGUSTINIAN-REFORMATION PARADIGM: MERIT CONNECTED TO ONTOLOGY

We have seen that a key difference between the traditional Augustinian paradigm and the republication position is a re-definition of the concept of merit. Why does this position find it necessary to redefine this concept? What drives them to see this as a necessary adjustment to Reformed theology? The key to understanding this redefinition lies in the role given to *ontology* in the definition of merit.

In the Augustinian paradigm of the Westminster Confession, the concept of merit is related not only to moral perfection but also to ontology. What is ontology all about? Simply put, ontology is concerned with a person's being or essential nature. Thus, onto-logical considerations lead to the clear distinction that the Bible makes between the being and essence of God, in contrast to the being and essence of man. God is divine; man is human. God is sovereign Creator; man is mere creature. The Bible reveals God to be the transcendent Creator who is infinite, eternal, and unchangeable. In stark contrast to God's nature, man is a finite creature. He was created from the dust, his existence begins in time and space, and his nature is mutable. Cornelius Van Til, who had a profound influence in the OPC, continually emphasized the importance of ontology in his teaching. He always kept the Creator-creature distinction at the forefront of the study and practice of theology and apologetics.[1]

In sum, we need to see clearly how there is a vast "ontological divide" between God and man. All humans are sons and daughters of Adam and therefore share a common human nature in distinction from God's divine nature. This truth has great bearing upon theology even apart from the consideration of the fall's impact on the distance between God and man. These ontological considerations have marked Reformed theology at every point, including its doctrine of merit.

The Effects of Ontology on the Reformed Paradigm

How does ontology impact our understanding of merit? The paradigm of the Westminster Standards defines merit in a way that keeps ontology central, in order to do justice to the biblical truth of the "ontological divide" between God and man. When we talk about merit being defined "ontologically," we mean that the possibility of a person meriting something before God is related to man's being and nature, both before and after the fall.

The Westminster Confession embodies Augustine's view that it is impossible for fallen man to merit anything before God. This impossibility is first clearly rooted in the ethical reality of man's sinful nature. Since the fall, man is incapable of doing any works which could stand before the righteous judgment of God: "All have turned aside; together they have become worthless; no one does

---

1. For more on merit and ontology, see McGrath, *Iustitia Dei*, 49ff.; see also Irons, "Redefining Merit," 259ff.

good, not even one . . . For all have sinned, and fall short of the glory of God" (Rom 3:12, 23). In addition to these ethical considerations, the Confession also grounds its rejection of human merits in ontological considerations.

> We cannot by our best works merit pardon of sin, or eternal life at the hand of God, by reason of the great disproportion that is between them and the glory to come; and the infinite distance that is between us and God, whom, by them, we can neither profit, nor satisfy for the debt of our former sins, but when we have done all we can, we have done but our duty, and are unprofitable servants: and because, as they are good, they proceed from his Spirit; and as they are wrought by us, they are defiled, and mixed with so much weakness and imperfection, that they cannot endure the severity of God's judgment.[2]

The above paragraph in the Confession highlights the impossibility of man's ability to merit anything not only because of man's demerit in light of the fall, but also because of ontological considerations. Even for regenerate believers whose works "proceed from his Spirit," there is still a "great disproportion" between even "our best works" and "the glory to come." There is a great ontological chasm—an "infinite distance"—between God and man. Because God is the Creator and man is sinful creature, even if we have "done all we can, we have done but our duty, and are unprofitable servants" (Luke 17:10).

What about the possibility of man meriting anything before his fall into sin? Reformed theologians, following Augustine's lead, have always kept the nature of God in view when answering this question. God is the incomparable Holy One, and is infinitely above man in his very being and nature. God is the Creator and man is the creature. Because of this, the historic Reformed view has maintained that man as mere creature, before the fall, simply owes God complete obedience as a servant in the service of his divine Master. Though created in God's image, the Reformed

---

2. WCF 16.5.

tradition has taught that God never owed man, according to nature, the reward of eternal life and communion with God.

If man is to earn or merit the reward of having God and life with him as his everlasting inheritance, then God must *voluntarily condescend* to man. This voluntary condescension is manifested in the covenant that God establishes with man, as stated in the Westminster Confession.

> The distance between God and the creature is so great, that although reasonable creatures do owe obedience unto him as their Creator, yet they could never have any fruition of him as their blessedness and reward, but by some voluntary condescension on God's part, which he hath been pleased to express by way of covenant.[3]

This is how Reformed theology, following the Augustinian tradition, has explained the way God has "bridged" the gap of the "great disproportion" between God and man. It is worth noting again how ontological considerations even before the fall have impacted the Reformed view of merit. According to the paradigm of the Westminster Standards, Adam's ability to merit the "fruition" of God as his "blessedness and reward" is dependent upon God's voluntary condescension. The Confession makes this doctrine *foundational* to the establishment of the covenant and the attainment of its reward.

The "Covenant Merit" of Adam

The doctrine of God's voluntary condescension goes hand in hand with the distinction that developed in Reformed theology between "covenanted" merit and "strict" or "proper" merit. *Covenant merit* is assigned to Adam in the covenant of works, whereas *strict merit* is assigned to Christ in the covenant of grace. What is the difference between the two? Covenant merit is a lesser category of merit when compared to strict merit. Adam's merit is said to be "improper" when it is measured against the standard of Christ's

3. Ibid., 7.1.

"proper" merit. This designation of *covenant merit* reflects the ontological considerations which pertain to Adam's status. It seeks to take into account the Creator-creature distinction and God's act of condescension[4] to enter into covenant with Adam. According to the Confession, the establishment of the covenant of works is God's appointed means of condescension, so that man as mere creature may know and enjoy God as his ultimate blessedness and reward.

Professor Cornel Venema explains how this lesser category of merit was deemed a necessary component of a biblical covenant theology.

> Due to the radical disproportion between the infinite Creator and the finite creature, the obedience of Adam to the moral law of God could never obtain for him anything more than the title of an "unworthy servant" who had merely performed his duty. Obedience to the law of God is required of man as a creature, but God was under no obligation by nature to grant Adam the fullness of glorified life upon the basis of his personal and perfect obedience. When God voluntarily condescended to enter a covenant with his image-bearer, Adam, he conferred upon him and his posterity a covenanted right to eternal life that was an unmerited favor. Admittedly, it may be misleading to speak of "grace" in the prelapsarian covenant relationship, since the Scriptures ordinarily reserve the term for an unmerited favor that God grants to sinners who have demerited his favor and deserve only condemnation and death. However, the traditional and consensus view of Reformed theologians is that the covenant of works was a voluntary condescension on God's part that could never be "merited" in the proper and strict sense of the term.[5]

Thus, Adam the creature simply owes his Creator his dutiful obedience. The hope of heaven with God is realized only by way of covenant. As Venema states, God "conferred upon him and his

4. Ibid.
5. Venema, review of *TLNF*, 95–96.

posterity a covenanted right to eternal life that was an unmerited favor." Perfect and personal obedience is the condition required for receiving the reward of eternal life in the context of the covenant. If Adam would fulfill the condition of the covenant, he may be said to have merited the reward according to the terms of the covenant (hence, "covenant merit"), which God condescended to establish after creation.

This "traditional and consensus view," of which Venema speaks, is found in a number of writers. A couple of examples may be mentioned here. Noted Dutch theologian, Herman Bavinck, reflects upon the impact which ontological considerations have had on a distinctly Reformed and Augustinian understanding of merit. In his *Reformed Dogmatics* he speaks in no uncertain terms about the reality of the great "ontological divide." He considers the matter of man's relationship to God, as well as merit, in light of ontology.

> A creature as such owes its very existence, all that it is and has, to God; it cannot make any claims before God, and it cannot boast of anything; it has no rights and can make no demands of any kind. There is no such thing as merit in the existence of a creature before God, nor can there be since the relation between the Creator and a creature radically and once-for-all eliminates any notion of merit. This is true after the fall but no less before the fall. Then too, human beings were creatures, without entitlements, without rights, without merit. When we have done everything we have been instructed to do, we are still unworthy servants (*douloi achreioi*, Luke 17:10).[6]

Francis Turretin also gives us a succinct summary, or the "last word," if you will, of confessional Reformed orthodoxy on this subject. He concludes:

> Hence also it appears that there is no merit properly so called of man before God, in whatever state he is placed.[7]

6. Bavinck, *Reformed Dogmatics*, 2:570.
7. Turretin, *Institutes*, 2:712.

The "Strict Merit" of Christ

The merit of Christ, in contrast to Adam's "covenant" or "improper" merit, falls uniquely into the category of "strict" or "proper" merit. Adam was a mere creature, and was dependent on God's voluntary condescension to enter into the covenant of works. Jesus Christ, the second and last Adam, is uniquely set apart in his role as the Mediator of the covenant of grace. In the incarnation, Jesus is by nature true God as well as true man. He possesses a sinless human nature, which would qualify him (like Adam) to perform perfect and personal obedience. But Christ was able to merit eschatological life in more than the "covenanted" sense. Our Savior, being the divine Son of God, is uniquely qualified to merit eternal life in the covenant of grace in the "strict" or "full" sense of the term.

This truth is implicitly taught in the Westminster Confession, where Christ is said to satisfy the justice of God and "purchase" (i.e., "merit") the eschatological reward of the covenant for his people.

> The Lord Jesus, by his perfect obedience, and sacrifice of himself, which he through the eternal Spirit, once offered up unto God, hath fully satisfied the justice of his Father; and purchased, not only reconciliation, but an everlasting inheritance in the kingdom of heaven, for those whom the Father hath given unto him.[8]

Note how the Confession speaks of the fact that Christ has *"fully satisfied the justice of His Father."* This language speaks of the significance of Christ's person as well as his work. His merits "fully satisfy" (*strictly* or *properly*) the demands of God's righteous judgment.

The Larger Catechism states even more explicitly that the "worth and efficacy" of Christ's work is founded upon his divine person.

> Q. 38. Why was it requisite that the mediator should be God?

8. WCF 8.5.

> A. It was requisite that the mediator should be God, that he might sustain and keep the human nature from sinking under the infinite wrath of God, and the power of death; give worth and efficacy to his sufferings, obedience, and intercession; and to satisfy God's justice, procure his favor, purchase a peculiar people, give his Spirit to them, conquer all their enemies, and bring them to everlasting salvation.

Note how the Catechism speaks of Christ's divine nature as "giv[ing] worth and efficacy to his sufferings [and] obedience." The value of his merit is rooted in his divine nature. In other words, Christ's merit is determined ontologically.

Turretin sets forth five conditions for "true merit," as he calls it. These five points explain why Adam's obedience did not meet the criteria for strict or true merit, but Christ's did.

> (1) That the "work be undue"—for no one merits by paying what he owes (Lk. 17:10), he only satisfies; (2) that it be ours—for no one can be said to merit from another; (3) that it be absolutely perfect and free from all taint—for where sin is, there merit cannot be; (4) that it be equal and proportioned to the reward and pay; otherwise it would be a gift, not merit (which Bellarmine himself acknowledges [ibid., 5.17, pp. 629–31] according to the meaning of the Council of Trent); (5) that the reward be due to such a work from justice—whence an "undue work" is commonly defined to be one that "makes a reward due in the order of justice."[9]

These criteria stand behind the theology of the Westminster Confession, as well as other creeds and confessions of the Reformed churches. As was evident in WCF 8.5, the importance of ontology is especially showcased in the church's teaching concerning the incomparable glory and infinite value of Christ's person and work.

---

9. Turretin, *Institutes*, 2:712. In his *Outlines of Theology*, A. A. Hodge follows Turretin (in the Augustinian tradition) in setting forth the necessary criteria for a meritorious work in the "strict" and "proper" sense of the term (527–28).

A shining example of ontology's theological imprint is seen in *The Canons of Dort* (head 2, articles 3–4), which embodies the integral relationship between Christ's being and his merit.

Article 3: The Infinite Value of Christ's Death

This death of God's Son is the only and entirely complete sacrifice and satisfaction for sins; it is of infinite value and worth, more than sufficient to atone for the sins of the whole world.

Article 4: Reasons for This Infinite Value

This death is of such great value and worth for the reason that the person who suffered it is—as was necessary to be our Savior—not only a true and perfectly holy man, but also the only begotten Son of God, of the same eternal and infinite essence with the Father and the Holy Spirit. Another reason is that this death was accompanied by the experience of God's anger and curse, which we by our sins had fully deserved.

Thus, within an Augustinian-Reformation paradigm, merit in the "strict" or "proper" sense is possible only for Christ. In his sinless, pre-fall condition, Adam was only capable of an improper "covenant merit." This was a "lesser" category of merit because it required God's voluntary condescension. Christ's merit is "strict" and "proper" merit because it does not require such condescension, as it is intrinsically infinite in worth and value because of Christ's divine nature. This is an important part of the surpassing glory and worth of our Savior! His merit is by definition greater than the potential merit of Adam. Both could perform perfect, personal obedience. However, because of his divine nature, only Christ's obedience was inherently worthy of the reward of eternal life.

It is clearer now why Augustine and the Reformed tradition have maintained that sinful man cannot merit anything before God, and why Adam's covenant merit must be distinguished from Christ's strict merit. Theological discourse always includes making careful distinctions. On the one hand, we must affirm the clear and undeniable biblical parallels between the two Adams (Rom 5:12ff.;

1 Cor 15:45) that are central to covenant theology (including the doctrine of justification). On the other hand, Reformed teaching has equally sought to do justice to important ontological differences between the two figures. These differences have governed the Reformed definition and understanding of merit in the creeds and confessions of the Church. This is not surprising, since Scripture itself is replete with these kinds of ontological considerations. To take just one example, consider the apostle Paul's doxology at the end of the first half of his epistle to the Romans:

> Oh, the depth of the riches and wisdom and knowledge of God! How unsearchable are his judgments and how inscrutable his ways! "For who has known the mind of the Lord, or who has been his counselor?" "Or who has given a gift to him that he might be repaid?" For from him and through him and to him are all things. To him be the glory forever. Amen. (Rom 11:33–36)

Note the ontological considerations that govern the apostle's formulation. God's wisdom and knowledge are infinite, surpassing the ability of finite man to fully and completely comprehend. God's being is absolute, as he is the one from whom, through whom, and to whom all things exist and have their being. Therefore, no mere creature can perform a work by which he can *inherently* obligate God—"who has given a gift to him that he might be repaid?" Whatever worship, service, or work we might offer to God is already owed to him. He alone is the Creator and Redeemer and we are his handiwork. To him alone belongs the glory forever.

7

Two Different Definitions of Merit (Part 2)

The Republication Paradigm

THE REPUBLICATION PARADIGM: MERIT DIVORCED FROM ONTOLOGY

In the Republication Paradigm, merit is not defined *ontologically*, but *covenantally*. This redefinition of merit (which will be explained below in more detail) is central and foundational to the doctrine of republication. Shepherd (along with Daniel Fuller and FV proponents) have formulated a theology that categorically rejects the concept of merit in God's covenantal arrangements. In so doing, they have appealed to the biblical principle of the ontological disproportion between man and God. Yet, they have rejected the traditional doctrine of the covenant of works. They have deemed the idea of Adam's merit to be an inconsistent compromise of the Reformation's insistence of salvation and eternal life by God's grace alone. We believe that Kline (among many others) was correct in expressing concern over the categorical rejection of Adamic merit and the merit of Christ. The Bible's two-Adam covenantal structure demands that we account for the unique theological parallel between the two Adams and their mutual ability to perform perfect, personal obedience. We believe this was done in a careful and theologically balanced way through the traditional distinction between "covenant merit" and "strict merit." By confusing or failing to account for these two, many have gone as far as to reject the merit of Christ. In part 1, we observed that Norman Shepherd did eventually reject the necessity of Christ's imputed active obedience, and thus undermined the doctrine of justification.

Nevertheless, in his reaction to Shepherd's pendulum swing away from the ideas of "merit" and the "covenant of works," we believe Kline swung the pendulum too far in the other direction (as was presented in part 1). Yet, the editors of *TLNF* have stated their position clearly; they agree with Kline's conviction that the republication view is necessary, and will better serve the church by guarding against the errors of Shepherd. Instead of seeking to recover what we regard to be the balanced and biblically faithful view of merit and the covenant of works in our Confession and other creeds of the Reformed church, Kline and many of his followers have found it necessary to reformulate these ideas *apart from ontological considerations*. In our view, the resulting paradigm has serious repercussions on other important elements in the Reformed system of doctrine.

The Klinean reformulation includes three key elements, which will be considered below, point by point.

1. The conflation of creation and covenant (essentially eliminating the logical distinction between the two).

2. The rejection of the necessity of God's voluntary condescension to establish the covenant with man.

3. The redefinition of merit and justice along covenantal lines to the exclusion of ontology.

1. Man Is in Covenant with God at the Moment of Creation

The Klinean republication view teaches that man was in covenant with God at the very moment of creation. This is an important shift from the traditional viewpoint. Ontological considerations demand that there be at least a logical distinction (rather than a chronological or historical sequence) between God's creating man and his entering into covenant with him. The republication teaching now erases this confessional distinction (which is based upon the "great disproportion" between the Creator and creature), and thereby turns God's providential work of establishing the covenant into an aspect of the work of creation. Thus, we may say that the *two* distinct acts have been *conflated* or *collapsed* into essentially *one* act in this new view. For all intents and purposes, the relationship between God and man is not first that of sovereign Creator over his finite creature, but is from the point of creation a relationship of "God-in-covenant-with-man." For Professor Kline and those who have followed his lead in the republication position, it is improper to even consider man's existence apart from covenant. Thus, man's covenantal status seems to "trump" his creaturely status. Professor Kline makes this clear in *Kingdom Prologue*.

> Man's creation as image of God meant, as we have seen, that the creating of the world was a covenant-making process. There was no original non-covenantal order of mere nature on which the covenant was superimposed. Covenantal commitments were given by the Creator in the very act of endowing the man-creature with the mantle of the divine likeness . . . The situation never existed in which man's future was contemplated or presented in terms of a static continuation of the original state of blessedness.[1]

A recent book, *Sacred Bond*, written on the popular level concerning Reformed covenant theology, has put the Klinean reformulation in simple terms.[2]

---

1. Kline, *Kingdom Prologue*, 92.
2. See the critical review, Engelsma, review of *Sacred Bond*, 117–22.

> *God is the one who made the covenant, and he did so at*
> *creation.* For Adam and Eve to be made in the image of
> God is for them to be in covenant with God.[3]

The obliteration of the distinction between creation and covenant is extremely significant for laying the foundation of a new paradigm of merit—one that is divorced from ontological considerations.

We have already observed that the Creator-creature distinction lies at the center of the doctrines of God, man, and of the covenant in the history of Reformed theology. This distinction is also central to the traditional understanding of merit, as the differences between Adam's covenant merit and Christ's strict merit rest on ontological factors. It is apparent that the adherents to the Republication Paradigm have followed Professor Kline in their departure from the tradition in this regard. Professor David Van-Drunen shows his agreement with Kline in *TLNF.*

> Meredith G. Kline (1922–2007) follows his Reformed predecessors closely in affirming the works principle operative in the covenant with Adam and in associating this works principle with the reality of the image of God. He resolves the ambiguity patent in many of his predecessors, however, by refusing to separate the act of creation in the image of God from the establishment of the covenant with Adam. For Kline, the very act of creation in God's image entails the establishment of the covenant, with its requirement of obedience and its prospect of eschatological reward or punishment . . . God's creating Adam in his image and the establishment of the covenant are aspects of the same act, and thus Adam's image-derived natural human knowledge that obedience brings eschatological life was at the very same time covenantal knowledge of a special relationship that he enjoyed with God.[4]

It is debatable whether Kline's "Reformed predecessors" actually taught this conflation of creation and covenant, and whether

---

3. Brown and Keele, *Sacred Bond,* 43, emphasis in original.
4. VanDrunen, "Natural Law," 291.

it is fair to characterize the tradition as having "ambiguity" on this point. In his review of *TLNF*, Venema seeks to set the record straight.

> VanDrunen's characterization of this "ambiguity" in historic Reformed theology is rather puzzling. There is little evidence that many covenant theologians in the orthodox period simply identified the covenant of works with man's creation in God's image and subjection to the moral law of God. Rather than being an ambiguity in Reformed covenant theology, the distinction (without separation) between the creation of man in God's image and the institution of the prelapsarian covenant of works is nearly the unanimous opinion of the covenant theologians of the sixteenth and seventeenth centuries. VanDrunen's claim that there is an ambiguity in Reformed covenant theology on this point is belied by the express language of the Westminster Confession of Faith, when it describes the covenant as a "voluntary condescension" on God's part. Rather than being an ambiguity in the history of Reformed covenant theology, the consensus opinion expressed in the Confession views the covenant of works as a sovereign and voluntary initiative of God.[5]

We will address the idea of "voluntary condescension" in the next point. Here, it is important to underscore that the *conflation* of creation and covenant within the republication position is a departure from the formulations of the Westminster Standards. What is clear in the Standards is that God "entered into" the covenant of works with man as the result of his work of providence, rather than from his work of creation. Shorter Catechism Q. 12 explicitly identifies the making of the covenant of works with Adam and Eve as a "special act of providence"—not an act that coincides or co-originates with the work of creation.[6] The Republication Paradigm rejects this formulation of the Standards when it teaches that the covenant relationship is an aspect of creation.

---

5. Venema, review of *TLNF*, 95.
6. See WSC 10.

2. Voluntary Condescension Is Eliminated

In the above quote, Venema shows that *voluntary condescension* is clearly affirmed within the mainstream Reformed position when he writes, "Rather than being an ambiguity in the history of Reformed covenant theology, the consensus opinion expressed in the Confession views the covenant of works as a sovereign and voluntary initiative of God." The Confession's articulation of the doctrine appears to be the obvious answer to any claims of "ambiguity" in the tradition. Westminster Confession of Faith 7.1 makes the doctrine of voluntary condescension *foundational* to God's covenant with man as an expression of how God bridged the gap of the "great disproportion" between God and man. The Confession indicates that this doctrine is integrally connected to man's hope of heaven. Even sinless man "could never have any fruition of [God] as their blessedness and reward" without voluntary condescension. One may wonder why *TLNF* is silent on this integral part of covenant theology. We believe this omission is consistent with the previous point (1 above).

Although the authors of *TLNF* do not explicitly reject WCF 7.1, as Kline did,[7] it becomes clear that this is the logical and necessary conclusion of Kline's viewpoint. Lee Irons wrote extensively about this in the article "Redefining Merit" for the Kline Festschrift.

> It is therefore incorrect to speak of God voluntarily condescending to the creature to make a covenant. For the very fact of creation itself has already constituted man in a covenant relationship with his creator. This formulation of the mutual reciprocity of creation and covenant shows more clearly than ever that the covenant of works is not a matter of grace but simple justice toward the creature made in God's image.[8]

It is evident that WCF 7.1 becomes problematic for the republication position. Even if an explicit rejection of God's voluntary condescension (such as the one by Irons) is absent in *TLNF*,

---

7. See part 1, chap. 4.
8. Irons, "Redefining Merit," 267.

an implicit one remains. The republication view's "erasure" of the historic distinction between the work of creation and the establishment of the covenant *necessarily* leads to the rejection of the doctrine. Irons has told us the reason in the above quote. Since the republication position entails that creation itself is conflated with the covenant relationship, there is no need (in this system) to bridge an ontological divide between God and man through voluntary condescension. As Irons clearly states, "For the very fact of creation itself has already constituted man in a covenantal relationship with his creator."

Thus, in the Republication Paradigm, the doctrine of condescension actually gets in the way. As is reflected in the quote from Irons, adherents of the republication view are concerned that the doctrine of voluntary condescension opens the door to Shepherd's error. How might this happen? Voluntary condescension would seem to allow for the claim that the covenant relationship between God and Adam is founded on love or grace rather than on a works principle ("simple justice"). This paradigm therefore rejects the idea that God's goodness, benevolence, or unmerited favor is foundational for the establishment of the covenant relationship. Such a rejection of voluntary condescension, in our view, is to throw out the proverbial baby with the bath water, and will lead to catastrophic alterations within the system of doctrine. One cannot remove a foundation stone ("voluntary condescension" in WCF 7.1) without a significant shift occurring—one that will inevitably damage the structure (covenant theology) resting upon it.

3. Merit and Justice Are Determined "Covenantally"

The previous two points lead to the third and final element of the Republication Paradigm shift. In light of the conflation of creation and covenant and the removal of voluntary condescension, it becomes evident that the historical Reformed concept of merit must be replaced with a new model. Merit must not be defined ontologically. Merit and justice are no longer to be governed by God's nature (ontology) or considered in light of the Creator-creature distinction. Nor is the distinction between strict and covenant merit a legitimate or relevant one to make. Instead, merit and justice are to be determined "covenantally." What does this mean in the republication view? Only the terms of a particular covenant may decide what is "just" and "meritorious." Merit, in this new paradigm, may be defined as follows: one performs a meritorious work when he fulfills the stated stipulation (i.e., condition or requirement) of a given law-covenant.

This might be confusing to some readers because this redefined notion of merit uses the term "covenant merit" in a novel way. This term has been used historically in one way, but is now being used with a different meaning. What are the precise differences between the Klinean version of "covenant merit" and the traditional view?

The traditional paradigm affirms that Adam's merit was considered to be covenant merit *in distinction from* strict merit. In other words, Adam's perfect obedience, as a creature, is being contrasted with Christ's obedience as the God-man. On the one hand, Adam's obedience was counted as *meritorious on the basis of the covenant* that had been established as an expression of God's voluntary condescension. He had the ability to perform perfect, personal obedience to the law as the ground of his reward. (This stands in contrast to the covenant of grace, which requires faith in Christ as the way of salvation.) However, Adam's finite works of obedience could never be considered as valuable as the infinite gift of eternal life. On the other hand, Christ's obedience could be counted as *strictly meritorious* since it was inherently worthy of receiving such a reward. Thus, the traditional definition of covenant merit is dependent on ontological considerations. In the traditional view, "covenant merit" only possessed meaning as it stood in contrast to "strict merit." It existed as part of a biblical and systematic theology that not only took into account the Creator-creature distinction, but viewed it as *foundational* for its theology. Nevertheless, strict and proper merit *did actually exist* in the history of redemption. It is hardly an example of theological abstraction or speculation that would detract from a concrete biblical theology of justice and merit. Instead, "strict merit" serves to uniquely identify the merits of Jesus Christ which were historically accomplished on behalf of his people, in the fulfillment of his active and passive obedience.

Within the new Republication Paradigm, "covenant merit" is used to communicate a different concept than what has been understood by the customary use of the term. The new use of "covenant merit" no longer serves to communicate the importance of the ontological divide between the Creator and creature. In fact, the Klinean-republication version of "covenant merit" is no longer based upon, defined by, or understood in reference to ontology at all. Points 1 and 2 above have laid the groundwork for understanding why the Republication Paradigm has removed all ontological considerations from the definition of merit. The pathway has been cleared for a new paradigm of merit.

A NEW MERIT PARADIGM BASED ON KLINE'S "SIMPLE JUSTICE"

In the republication view, merit is defined in terms of God's revealed will as specified by the terms of the covenant. Simply stated, merit is whatever God says it is. According to the republication position, the nature of the specified condition is ultimately irrelevant for determining its meritorious or non-meritorious character. The condition may be perfection (as in the covenant with Adam), or it may be something less than perfection (as in the Mosaic covenant). A work is meritorious, therefore, simply when God decides to accept it as such through the stated stipulations or conditions of a particular covenantal arrangement. Kline referred to this as *simple justice*.

> In keeping with the nature of God's covenant with Adam as one of simple justice, covenant theology holds that Adam's obedience in the probation would have been the

performing of a meritorious deed by which he earned
the covenanted blessings.[9]

If God gives a particular condition in a particular covenant,
and that condition is met through obedience, then it is a matter
of God's *simple justice* that he reward that obedience as meritorious. As Kline says elsewhere, "God's covenant Word is definitive
of Justice."[10] Note what follows. In this redefined view of merit,
there is no longer any need or place for the previous distinction
made between Adam's *covenant merit* in contrast to Christ's *strict
merit*. In terms of the definition of merit, Adam and Christ can
equally earn the rewards of their respective covenants according to
the principle of simple justice.

It is also important to note another ramification of this new
paradigm. Just as the respective obedience of Adam and Christ
would be deemed *equally* meritorious according to the definition of "simple justice," so also the works of others, beyond (or
between) the two federal heads, may *equally* be counted as meritorious. The Republication Paradigm allows for only *one category
or definition of merit* ("covenant merit") which is applied equally
to Adam, to Christ, *as well as to other figures after the fall* (such as
Noah, Abraham, and Israel). This explains why meritorious works
of obedience are possible for sinners between Adam and Christ in
this new paradigm. The redefinition of merit "allows" God to make
an additional meritorious arrangement outside of those made with
the two Adams. After the fall, in the Mosaic covenant, for example,
God may decide to make an arrangement in which he promises
temporal-typological blessings on the basis of Israel's imperfect,
sincere, national obedience, instead of the perfect, entire, and personal obedience which was required of the two covenant heads
(see following diagram).

9. Kline, "Covenant Theology" (unpublished version), para. 9.

10. Kline, *God, Heaven and Har Magedon*, 64.

The redefinition of "covenant merit" does not require any ontological considerations. In fact, it does not even require moral perfection on the part of man. Thus, the fact that Israel's works are those of fallen sinful creatures is completely irrelevant. They are meritorious because God says so. All that matters is that they fulfill God's covenant Word, which alone defines and determines what constitutes merit and justice in any given covenantal arrangement.

8

The Redefinition of Merit and the Two Levels of the Mosaic Covenant

THREE MODIFICATIONS OF THE MOSAIC COVENANT

We have seen how the republication position, particularly as it is advocated by Kline and some of his followers, is marked by a clear departure from traditional covenant theology. In the previous chapter, we considered the reformulations made to creation and covenant, voluntary condescension, and the definition of merit. All of these things have to do with the *foundations* of covenant theology, as historically formulated.

How do these departures from traditional covenant theology shape the Republication Paradigm's view of the Mosaic covenant? In the first part of this chapter, we are going to outline and consider three key features of this position:

1. The division of the covenant into upper and lower levels.

2. The elevation of Israel to the status of being a "corporate Adam" that undergoes a "covenant-of-works probation" analogous to the first and last Adam.

3. The "pedagogical purpose" of this meritorious works probation within the temporal and typological sphere of Israel's corporate existence.

1. The Division of the Mosaic Covenant into Upper and Lower Levels

Lower ("Order of Salvation") Level

In the republication view, the Mosaic covenant must be divided into two distinct levels. The *lower-foundational level* deals with spiritual blessings, particularly the eternal salvation of the individual believer, which is by grace through faith in the Christ who was to come. It is important to underscore that adherents of the Republication Paradigm clearly assert that fallen man is unable to merit any spiritual or eternal blessings. It is also clear from their writings that eternal salvation is always granted to fallen man on the basis of Christ's person and work, and received by grace through faith alone. Thus, Israel could not merit eternal blessings. This foundational level is sometimes referred to as the *ordo salutis* level, or *order of salvation* level. The order of salvation (effectual calling, regeneration, faith, justification, etc.) remains the same in every epoch of the covenant of grace, including the time of the Mosaic covenant.

Upper ("History of Salvation") Level

Nevertheless, the republication view also teaches that the Mosaic covenant is more than *simply* a covenant of grace. Instead, this covenant contains a more complex combination of works and grace in its administration. It has a second, *upper-typological level* that is overlaid on the foundational level of grace. This level is sometimes referred to as the *historia salutis* or *history of salvation* level. In contrast to the underlying *ordo salutis* level, the republication doctrine affirms that Israel's national obedience functions, within the history of salvation, as a type of the work of Christ. This upper level of the Mosaic covenant governs the temporal life of the nation of Israel in the promised land. On this level, the republication viewpoint allows for the possibility of fallen man to merit temporal blessings. Israel as a nation is said to have been under a principle of meritorious works in order to retain their place in the land, which is a type of the kingdom of heaven. If Israel obeyed, she would be blessed on the basis of her meritorious works. If she disobeyed, she would earn the curses of God, culminating in the exile of the nation from the land. These two levels in the Mosaic covenant, which are set forth by the authors of *TLNF*, are based on the formulation of Meredith Kline.

> Classic covenantalism recognizes that the old Mosaic order (at its foundation level—that is, as a program of individual salvation in Christ) was in continuity with previous and subsequent administrations of the overarching covenant of grace. But it also sees and takes at face value the massive Biblical evidence for a peculiar discontinuity present in the old covenant in the form of a principle of meritorious works, operating not as a way of eternal salvation but as the principle governing Israel's retention of its provisional, typological inheritance.[1]

It is worth noting how the temporal, upper level gives the Mosaic covenant the character of a *law covenant* instead of the character of the *promissory covenant* made with Abraham. This is why we may say that the republication view of the Mosaic covenant is more than simply a covenant of grace in its nature or character. On the underlying foundational level, there is continuity with what comes before and after Moses in the covenant of grace. On the upper level, governed by the works principle, there is discontinuity. On this level, the Mosaic covenant stands in line with the works (law) covenant with Adam before the fall, and is antithetical to the nature or character of the Abrahamic covenant (as well as other administrations of the covenant of grace).

---

1. Kline, "Gospel until the Law," 434.

2. The Nation of Israel as a "Corporate Adam"

The second distinctive development of the republication view of the Mosaic covenant is that Israel is seen as a "corporate Adam" that undergoes a reenactment of the first Adam's probation. The original covenant of works arrangement is republished "in some sense" in the Mosaic covenant. Like Adam in the garden, the nation of Israel is put into a garden (the land of Canaan) and undergoes an analogous trial of probation. Israel, like Adam, is put in the position of having to merit the reward of the covenant. On the upper level of the Republication Paradigm, Israel's obedience has nothing to do with earning the reward of eschatological life. Her meritorious obedience would only retain the physical and temporal inheritance in the land of Canaan.

The editors of *TLNF* regularly appeal to the "corporate Adam" theme in their defense of their formulation of the republication doctrine.

> We should not miss the implied comparison between Adam and Israel, in that both transgressed expressly revealed command . . . Succinctly stated, both of God's sons, Adam and Israel, lived under *nomos*-governed circumstances.[2]

One of the editors, David VanDrunen, also speaks directly and extensively of "Israel's Adamic Identity" as he affirms Israel's placement within a probationary covenant of works.[3] This viewpoint is far from unique to the authors of *TLNF*. They are joined by the authors of *Sacred Bond* in promoting a meritorious arrangement and "corporate Adam" identity for Israel in the republication view of the Mosaic covenant.

> Just as Adam had to obey to earn the reward of the covenant, so Israel had to keep the law to earn the blessings

---

2. *TLNF*, 9.

3. See VanDrunen, "Israel's Recapitulation of Adam's Probation," 304ff.

of the covenant. Obedience to the law was the means
whereby they both obtained the reward.[4]

Putting these things together, we are now in a better position
to understand the republication view's understanding of Israel's
function. The nation, in her Adamic capacity, is said to serve a
"pedagogical purpose" in the history of redemption.

3. Corporate Israel's Upper Level "Pedagogical Purpose"

According to the proponents of the republication view, the purpose
of Israel's "Adamic" status and situation is to serve a *pedagogical*
(i.e., instructive) *purpose*. Israel is placed in a situation of meriting
an earthly inheritance to clearly *teach* that she is ultimately unable
to obey God's law, cannot earn eternal salvation by her works, and
needs the imputation of Christ's active obedience.

To say that Israel's meritorious obedience serves a *pedagogical purpose* is a significant modification of the way that Reformed
covenant theology has understood the pedagogical function of the
law. This pedagogical or "schoolmaster" function is based on Paul's
words in Galatians 3:24: "Wherefore the law was our schoolmaster
to bring us unto Christ, that we might be justified by faith" (KJV).
Traditionally, the designation of the law as "guardian," "tutor" or
"schoolmaster," refers to the law's function as a clear revelation of
God's perfect moral standard of righteousness. Since fallen man
is unable to fulfill the demands of the moral law, which requires
perfect conformity to God's righteousness, the law serves as a
schoolmaster when it comes to the matter of justification. The law's
perfect demands direct us to faith in Christ (instead of our own
law keeping), since he alone is able to perfectly keep the law and
satisfy the demands of God's justice for his people.

In the Republication Paradigm, it is now stated that the requirement of meritorious obedience for Israel becomes a type of
Christ's obedience (in effect, like Adam). It is no longer strictly the
moral law itself, with its *unchanging universal demands*, that serves

4. Brown and Keele, *Sacred Bond*, 111.

as a *schoolmaster* leading us to Christ. Instead, the pedagogical function of the law has become subtly redefined by Kline and the authors of *TLNF*. They have reinterpreted Paul's words to mean that the *demand for meritorious works in the Mosaic covenant* is the schoolmaster that leads us to Christ's active obedience. The meritorious works operating on the temporal, upper-typological level thus serves the covenant of grace. How does it do this? We are told that the Israelite is to learn from his failure to merit blessings in the land that he needs a Savior who alone will merit eternal blessings for him. These blessings are offered and conferred in accordance with the principle of grace on the lower-foundational, spiritual-eternal level of the covenant. Once Christ comes, the temporal, upper level within the Mosaic covenant ends. At that point in salvation history, the typological function of Israel has reached its fulfillment in the establishment of the new covenant.

The two levels of the Mosaic covenant, as affirmed in the republication view, may be set forth by way of summary in the following table.

Mosaic Covenant's Two Levels	Nature/Character	Principle of Inheritance
Upper-typological (*Historia salutis*)	Temporal-Typological Blessings (in land of Canaan) for Israel as "corporate Adam"	By Meritorious Works of Obedience to stipulations of Mosaic covenant
Lower-foundational (*Ordo salutis*)	Spiritual-Eternal Blessings (salvation/heaven) for individual believers among Israel	By Grace through faith in Jesus Christ, the Mediator of the covenant of grace

THE OUTWORKING OF THE REPUBLICATION PARADIGM

Following Kline's lead, *TLNF* asserts that the Mosaic covenant is *in some sense* a republication of the covenant of works with Adam. In what sense? So far, it is clear that they are under a covenant of works in the sense that both Adam's and Israel's obedience can merit blessings from God. For Adam it was *eternal* blessing. For Israel, it was *temporal* blessing.

Did Israel actually merit blessing? There seems to be some confusion or disagreement on this point. According to some adherents of the republication teaching, the ability to earn temporal blessings from God appears to be *unrealized*, as they maintain that Israel actually failed to earn blessings by her works.

> God demanded of his son Israel obedience to his law to merit the blessings of the covenant. If Israel could earn the earthly blessings by their obedience, then there might be a chance for fallen man to earn his way to heaven. Yet generation after generation, Israel failed miserably.[5]

For others, including at least two of the editors of *TLNF*, it seems that Israel prospered for a time in the land of Canaan and *did* realize temporal blessings by their obedience. Later, their disobedience brought God's cursing, leading to the exile.

> In the context of the Old Testament itself, there is often the assumption that the law can be kept in some measure and indeed has been kept by certain generations, such as the generation of Joshua and Caleb.[6]

> God did not enforce the works principle strictly and in fact taught his OT people something about the connection of obedience and blessing by giving them, at times, temporal reward for relative (imperfect) obedience.[7]

Did the Israelites actually obtain any blessings by their meritorious works or not? Ultimately, this question misses the heart of the issue. Problems still persist. In the end, whether or not blessings were actually secured, Israel is under a paradigm in which they could. Thus, the Republication Paradigm itself is a significant departure from the Augustinian-Reformed paradigm.

This concern involves more than Israel's potential fulfillment or non-fulfillment of the typological works-probation. The Republication Paradigm also concerns *God's ability* to make an

5. Ibid., 117–18.

6. Estelle, "Leviticus 18:5," 118n45.

7. VanDrunen, "Natural Law," 301n30.

arrangement in which he makes himself indebted to sinful man. The question does not merely concern whether or not actual blessings were granted according to Kline's "simple justice," but whether God's *infinite justice* would allow it. Even if one rejects the notion that Israel actually merited blessings from God, a proponent of the republication doctrine is still left with this question: "How can God make a covenant of works with sinners in which he must lower the bar of his righteousness and accept imperfect obedience as the basis for earning his favor?" Even if this divine favor would consist of nothing more than temporal-typological blessings (as opposed to eternal blessings), this favor would still be granted historically (i.e., really, not typologically) on the basis of works, and not of grace. The terms of the Mosaic covenant are described as being in sharp antithesis to the gracious terms of the Abrahamic covenant. Thus, regardless of whether or not Israel actually fulfilled the terms to receive any blessing, the Mosaic covenant is governed by a paradigm of merit, which would obligate God to reward sinful works with blessing, according to his "simple justice." This simply does not add up, when considered in light of the customary biblical view of God's justice, which is based on ontological considerations.

The outworking of the Klinean paradigm in the Mosaic covenant makes several things clear within the context of the history of covenant theology. This two-level construction of the Mosaic covenant is only possible because the historical Reformed view of merit has been replaced by a new paradigm. It is clear that this new paradigm is foundational for the entire republication view. Furthermore, by removing all ontological considerations, this redefinition of merit permits what the traditional view has rejected, namely, the possibility of any type of meritorious accomplishment by fallen man. In the historic Augustinian-Reformed paradigm, God can never be placed in a sinner's debt. He can never be in a position or enter into a covenantal arrangement which requires that he reward or bless the sin-tainted works of fallen man according to the principle of his absolute and perfect justice.

CONCLUSION OF PART 2

Such a redefinition of merit is bound to have far reaching implications. It is the contention of the present writers that the new paradigm of merit employed in the republication view is ultimately theologically unstable. Therefore, the call of *TLNF*, asking the church to embrace its republication teaching, ought to be carefully weighed and considered in light of established confessional terms and definitions. We believe that the Republication Paradigm significantly recasts traditional concepts and alters the landscape of covenant theology, as expressed in and defined by the Westminster Standards. Highlighting some of the effects caused by the instability of the paradigm will be the task of part 3.

PART 3

The Instability of the Republication Paradigm

The thesis or aim of *The Law Is Not of Faith* is to show "that the covenant of works is in some sense republished in the Mosaic covenant at Sinai."[8] The authors of *TLNF* seek to demonstrate that the phrase "in some sense" is a simple way of tying together the various strands of the Reformed tradition on this issue. Although the phrase "in some sense" may seem harmless enough, this language is ambiguous, lacks necessary precision, and thus leads to theological confusion.

Where the Westminster Confession speaks about the relationship between the Adamic and Mosaic eras, it does so clearly and without ambiguity. What is affirmed in our tradition is the commonly held understanding that the same *moral law* given to Adam has been "republished" at Sinai in the Ten Commandments. Robert Strimple, retired professor of systematic theology at WSC, has made this very point.

> All we Reformed believers are "republicationists" in the sense that we all believe the moral law of God was reaffirmed—summarized or "republished" if you will—on Mt. Sinai. We have no argument there. The point at issue

8. *TLNF*, 6.

> is whether or not that moral law was reaffirmed/repub-
> lished on Mt. Sinai *as in some sense the covenant of works
> made with Adam.*[9]

The traditional, confessional view is very different from the republication position found in *TLNF*. As Mark Jones states:

> To argue that the giving of the law at Sinai has simi-
> larities with the covenant of works is not, to my mind,
> controversial in Reformed circles. To argue that a meri-
> torious works-principle operated at the typological level
> in the Mosaic covenant—because Sinai is viewed as a law
> covenant—is, however, a serious point of contention.[10]

The republication viewpoint, therefore, replaces the notion of
a "republication" or "reaffirmation" of the unchanging moral law
at Sinai with an alternate conception. Our concerns are pointedly
focused on those who use the phrase "in some sense" to communicate the idea that a meritorious works paradigm is "republished"
in the Mosaic covenant on the typological level.

Furthermore, *TLNF* argues that the republication viewpoint
"in some sense" is the predominant or mainstream view in the history of Reformed covenant theology. As the editors state:

> In classic historic Reformed theology, despite the var-
> iegated expression, the same thread runs throughout,
> namely, the idea that in some sense the covenant of works
> was repeated or republished in the Mosaic covenant.[11]

However, we share the concerns of notable historical theologians who have argued that the history of theology simply does
not support this contention. Attempting to catalog all the precise
and nuanced differences among Reformed theologians is beyond
the scope of this book. We encourage a careful study of the original
sources. Nevertheless, it may be helpful to note one example of the
kind of assessment being made about the historical claims found
in *TLNF*. Cornel Venema makes an important point.

9. Strimple, "Westminster Confession of Faith," 4.

10. Jones, review of *TLNF*, 120.

11. *TLNF*, 13.

I do not believe this interpretation of the history of the development of Reformed covenant theology can stand up to careful historical scrutiny. The majority opinion of Reformed theologians of the orthodox period, and one that is codified in the Westminster Confession of Faith, is that there are two covenants, the covenant of works and covenant of grace, that are *substantially* different . . . Though it is difficult to determine the pedigree of the version of the republication thesis with which the authors of *The Law Is Not of Faith* identify, it seems to be a view that finds its origins more in the recent writings of Meredith Kline than in the writings of theologians of the orthodox period.[12]

Note again how Venema contrasts the pedigree of the majority opinion of Reformed theologians with the recent writings of Meredith Kline. Furthermore, he makes clear that the predominant view has been "codified" in the Westminster Confession of Faith.

With this in view, it is perhaps clearer why the phrase "in some sense" is unhelpful and even misleading. It can easily become a smoke screen that shields the reader from this important historical reality: The church has in its possession a carefully crafted and long-established consensus viewpoint that has emerged from the historical discussion on the covenants. The creeds and confessions of the Reformed churches have carefully defined *exactly in what sense* a covenant may be called a covenant of works or covenant of grace, and *exactly* how merit, justice and good works are to be defined. To argue that the Reformed tradition can affirm that the Mosaic covenant is *in some undefined sense* a covenant of works belies the truth that there is already a clearly defined understanding of Scripture's teaching in our hands. To simply reiterate the "in some sense" thesis constitutes a failure to demonstrate the precise way in which the republication view accords with the clear consensus view of the Westminster Standards. In order for true progress to be made in this dialogue, it must be recognized that this is the point of contention with the republication thesis.

12. Venema, review of *TLNF*, 100.

Therefore, to refer to the Mosaic covenant *in any sense* as a republication *of the covenant of works* invites members of a confessional church to compare that position with the church's Standards. When one compares the two, we believe it becomes evident that the Republication Paradigm uses traditional language and concepts, but redefines them in the service of its own paradigm. Not only do these new definitions fail to harmonize with those contained in the Westminster Standards, they may lead to other systematic changes in our confessional theology.

In part 3, we will show how the redefinition of merit and the division of the Mosaic covenant into two levels lead to an unstable theological paradigm. The causes for instability in the Republication Paradigm will be set forth and discussed according to the following four divisions.

- Chapter 9: The Republication Paradigm's view of the Mosaic covenant entails a departure from the confessional definition of the covenant of works.

- Chapter 10: The Republication Paradigm alters the nature of the Mosaic covenant as a covenant of grace by combining the incompatible principles of works and grace within a single covenant.

- Chapter 11: The Republication Paradigm redefines merit and justice, creating theological confusion and instability for other key elements within our system of doctrine.

- Chapter 12: The Republication Paradigm alters the Reformed understanding of what constitutes a good work.

In these four chapters, we will raise questions and argue points that we believe warrant further consideration.

9

The Covenant of Works and the Republication Paradigm

THE DEFINITION OF THE COVENANT OF WORKS IN THE WESTMINSTER STANDARDS

What does the Westminster Confession of Faith say concerning the *essential* parts or elements of the covenant of works? The essential or constituent parts of a covenant determine its essence, substance, or nature. These are set forth in chapter 7, "Of God's Covenant with Man." The covenant of works is that first covenant

> wherein life was promised to Adam; and in him to his posterity, upon condition of perfect and personal obedience.[1]

What is the condition or stipulation required of Adam in the covenant of works? It is "personal, entire, exact, and perpetual obedience" to God's law[2] including the command forbidding Adam to eat of the tree of the knowledge of good and evil, upon pain of

1. WCF 7.2; see also 19.1.
2. Ibid., 19.1.

death.[3] What is the reward promised in the covenant of works, if Adam should fulfill the condition? The reward is life, and this is understood to be speaking about eternal life, "of which the tree of life was a pledge."[4] WCF 7.1 supports this idea that the reward in view is eternal life. Here, the Confession speaks of God's voluntary condescension in establishing the covenant and the possibility of man having the "fruition of Him [God] as their blessedness and reward." To have the fruition of God as one's reward is implicitly to have eternal (not merely temporal) life. Thus, the covenant of works has two essential elements: (1) the requirement or condition of perfect, personal, and perpetual obedience; and (2) the promise or reward of eternal life.

THE "COVENANT OF WORKS" TERMINOLOGY IN THE REPUBLICATION PARADIGM

When one comes to the republication doctrine, which claims to be within the sphere of the Reformed tradition, there is an expectation that the standard definition and use of the term "covenant of works" would be maintained. However, in the Republication Paradigm, the label "covenant of works" is being used in the service of another arrangement between God and Israel on a temporal-typological level within the Mosaic covenant.[5] In the following quotations, we see evidence that the two essential components of the Westminster definition of the covenant of works with Adam (1 and 2 above) have been altered in the Republication Paradigm.

> In other words, in some sense, the covenant of works was republished at Sinai. It was not republished, however, as the covenant of works per se, but as part of the covenant

3. WSC 12.

4. WLC 20. See also Gen 3:22; Rev 22:2; WCF 7.1.

5. Kline acknowledges that this is the case: "Within the limitations of the fallen world and with modifications peculiar to the redemptive process, the old theocratic kingdom was a reproduction of the original covenantal order. Israel as the theocratic nation was mankind stationed once again in a paradise-sanctuary, under probation in a covenant of works" (*Kingdom Prologue*, 352).

of grace, which pointed to the person and the work of Christ.[6]

But the demand for sincere obedience, relative obedience (albeit imperfect) which would showcase an appropriate measure of readable obedience before the surrounding nations, has passed . . . Israel had served her purpose.[7]

Flawless obedience was the condition of Adam's continuance in the Garden; but Israel's tenure in Canaan was contingent on the maintenance of a measure of religious loyalty which needed not to be comprehensive of all Israel nor to be perfect even in those who were the true Israel.[8]

God did not enforce the works principle strictly and in fact taught his OT people something about the connection of obedience and blessing by giving them, at times, temporal reward for relative (imperfect) obedience.[9]

Note especially how both the condition and the reward promised are described in the republication of the covenant of works under Moses. God is said merely to require a *measure of sincere, relative, imperfect, and national religious loyalty or obedience*, in order to gain a *temporal reward* of continuing tenure in the promised land.

THE UNSTABLE RESULTS OF THE REPUBLICATION PARADIGM

It is evident that there are key differences between the historical usage of the term "covenant of works," as defined by the Westminster Standards, and the way this label is being employed within the

6. *TLNF*, 11.
7. Estelle, "Leviticus 18:5," 137.
8. Ibid., quoting Kline, 137n120.
9. VanDrunen, "Natural Law," 301n30.

Republication Paradigm. As we discuss the theological instability of the Republication Paradigm with respect to the covenant of works, we will focus our analysis on three key points.

1. The nature of the condition in the covenant of works.

2. The nature of the reward in the covenant of works.

3. The moral nature of man in the covenant of works.

1. The Nature of the Condition in the Covenant of Works

In the Republication Paradigm, the nature of the condition or requirement of obedience in a covenant of works has been altered.

- Obedience is no longer *perfect*: In the Republication Paradigm, God is said to merely require "imperfect," "sincere," or "relative" obedience of Israel.

- Obedience is no longer *personal*: Adam was *personally* required to obey the condition of perfect obedience for himself and his posterity. In the Republication Paradigm, Israel's *corporate obedience* was to function as the meritorious grounds for obtaining blessings in the land.

- Obedience is no longer *perpetual*: Adam was disqualified from the reward of life since he did not *continue* in his exact and entire (perfect) obedience before God. In the case of Israel, there seems to be allowance for a fluctuation of obedience during hundreds of years in their "probation." Unlike Adam's case, it is unclear at what precise point in time Israel's obedience would fail to live up to the typological standards, and her disobedience would merit the punishment of exile.

Thus, the traditional understanding of the condition required in a covenant of works is redefined in the republication teaching. The Republication Paradigm is now attributing to a "covenant of works" under Moses the kind of obedience (imperfect and sincere) that the Confession says belongs to the covenant of grace.[10] Does not God's acceptance of imperfect, relative obedience (which falls

10. See WCF 16.5–6.

short of the glory of God) necessarily demand the presence of pure grace, in contrast to and apart from works?

How can Israel's imperfect obedience, which is inherently demeritorious, (and thus deserving of God's judgment) be called meritorious and thus properly belong to a covenant of works? The republication designation of the Mosaic covenant as a "covenant of works" is thus improper and confusing because the traditional covenantal distinctions between works and grace are blurred. Merit is now attributed to the condition of imperfect and national works, whereas the Confession only attributes merit in a covenant of works to the perfect, personal, and perpetual obedience of the two Adams.

2. The Nature of the Reward in the Covenant of Works

In the Republication Paradigm, the nature of the reward or promise offered in a covenant of works arrangement has been modified. The reward is no longer eternal life, but temporal life. In the Westminster Standards, the reward or inheritance of the covenant is eternal life for Adam (and Christ). To insert another covenant of works arrangement that offers a reward of temporal life on the basis of meritorious works is foreign to our Standards. The Republication Paradigm is confusing because traditional covenant theology maintains a singular goal or reward of the covenant relationship (i.e., eternal life), whether it be in the context of the pre-fall covenant of works or the post-fall covenant of grace.[11]

3. The Moral Nature of Man in the Covenant of Works

In the Republication Paradigm, the moral nature of man required in a covenant of works has also changed. According to the Confession, a covenant of works can only be enacted with "sinless man" in his created state (before the fall). It is impossible for God to renew a covenant of works with fallen man. By his fall, man has "made

11. Ibid., 7.2–3.

himself incapable of life by that covenant [of works]."[12] Scripture clearly demonstrates fallen man's total depravity and complete inability (e.g., Rom 3:10ff.; 8:7, 8). If man in his pristine condition did not keep the covenant of works, it is a forgone conclusion that fallen man could never begin to keep it.

Nevertheless, the Republication Paradigm seems to elevate fallen man to a position in which he may overcome the consequences of the fall. It does this by viewing fallen Israel as being qualified to enter into a covenant of works again—a covenant in which (according to the traditional definition) God's law and character still demand perfect obedience. However, man's depraved, corrupt nature was inherited from Adam as the *punishment* for breaking the covenant of works.[13] To argue that God can once again reenact the Adamic arrangement as a meritorious arrangement with a group of sinners is to deny the reality of the penalty that God pronounced and conferred upon man when he broke that original arrangement. (It's as if God could arbitrarily change his mind, go against his previous judgment, and enter into a covenant of works with sinners whom he had previously deemed to be disqualified from such a covenant.) In this way, not only has the definition of a covenant of works changed, but God's faithfulness to his own Word or verdict is called into question.

As the Confession teaches, it is the very reality of man's *depraved nature* that necessitates the making of a second kind of covenant after the fall. The covenant of grace must use a very different method for obtaining the reward—namely, by grace through faith in the Mediator, Jesus Christ. Note how the broken covenant of works *requires* that an essentially gracious covenant arrangement be made with sinners for salvation and life.[14] In the Republication Paradigm, man's fallen condition no longer *necessitates* that a covenant between God and man be *essentially governed* by grace alone. Rather, God is "able" to renew and reenact the broken covenant of works which is *essentially governed* by a works-merit paradigm.

12. Ibid., 7.3.
13. See WSC 16, 18; WCF 6.3–4.
14. See WCF 7.3; 16.5; 19.6.

Yet, according to the Confession, such a works arrangement with Israel would be impossible, because it would be made with people who are already totally depraved, and unable to keep it. Although the Republication Paradigm claims to reinforce the necessity of God's grace after the fall, it actually produces theological instability by introducing after the fall a meritorious-works principle that is contrary to grace. In classic covenant theology, such a principle (after the fall) is reserved for the perfect works of Christ alone, performed on behalf of his sinful people.

10

The Nature of the Mosaic Covenant
and the Republication Paradigm

THE NATURE OF THE MOSAIC COVENANT IN THE
WESTMINSTER STANDARDS

Reformed theology has drawn a clear line of distinction between
the pre-fall covenant of works and the post-fall covenant of grace.
Theological confusion and incoherence results when the essential
elements of one covenant are mixed with the essential elements of
another in a single covenant.

How does the Westminster Confession of Faith define the *essential* elements of the covenant of grace? The following definition
is given in chapter 7, "Of God's Covenant with Man." The covenant
of grace is that second covenant

> wherein he freely offereth unto sinners life and salvation
> by Jesus Christ; requiring of them faith in him, that they
> may be saved, and promising to give unto all those that
> are ordained unto eternal life his Holy Spirit, to make
> them willing, and able to believe.[1]

1. WCF 7.3.

What is the condition or stipulation required of sinners in the covenant of grace? It is "faith in [Jesus Christ]." What is the reward promised in the covenant of grace, if sinners should fulfill the condition? The reward is eternal "life and salvation by Jesus Christ." Thus, the covenant of grace by definition has two essential elements in all its administrations: (1) the requirement or condition of faith in Jesus Christ; and (2) the promise or reward of salvation by Jesus Christ and eternal life.

It is worth underscoring how the Confession prevents the condition of faith from becoming a "good work" that merits the reward of life and salvation. In the covenant of grace, in contrast to the covenant of works, the requirement or stipulation of the covenant is graciously bestowed on the sinner. The reward of eternal life is obtained in essentially different ways in each covenant. The conditions of each covenant are mutually exclusive. Since the fall, the condition of the covenant can no longer be perfect obedience because man is totally depraved. He is unable to perform even a single work that meets the standard of God's perfect righteousness. Thus, the essential parts of the covenant of grace are *all* of grace, in contrast to works; the two can't be mixed.

The Mosaic Covenant as a Covenant of Grace

How do the Westminster Standards conceive of the covenant with Moses? It is clear that the Mosaic covenant is an administration of the covenant of grace. This means that the Mosaic covenant has the same *essential* parts as the Abrahamic or the New Testament administrations of the covenant of grace (1 and 2 above). In the current discussion, it is important to establish the *essential unity and continuity* among all the administrations of the covenant of grace—in both the Old and New Testaments—from Abraham to Moses to Christ. Although the Israelites learned through types and shadows, they were instructed and built up in faith in the same "promised Messiah, by whom they had full remission of sins, and eternal salvation."[2] This is why *every administration* of the covenant of grace (i.e., whether it be the Abrahamic, Mosaic, or New covenant) is gracious in its substance or essential character. What conclusion may be drawn? Chapter 7 of the Confession ends with this conclusion, "There are not therefore two covenants of grace, differing in substance, but one and the same, under various dispensations."[3] The Confession prohibits the idea that the Mosaic covenant (despite its legal content) is another type of covenant "differing in substance" from other administrations of "one and the same" covenant of grace. Therefore, when the Confession affirms that the Mosaic covenant is in essence a covenant of grace, it implies that it cannot in any way be in substance a covenant of works.

The Gracious Function of the Law in the Mosaic Covenant

What about the role of the law? The Larger Catechism explicitly identifies the gracious nature of the Mosaic covenant in the gracious function of the law in the life of Israel. In Q. 101, at the very point of the giving of the law, the Catechism so wonderfully draws out the significance of the "preface to the ten commandments." The law is given to Moses in the context of the accomplishment of God's gracious redemption of his people by the Passover lamb (Exod 12). We are therefore to learn, in the words of the Catechism,

> that he is a God in covenant, as with Israel of old, so with all his people; who, as he brought them out of their bondage in Egypt, so he delivereth us from our spiritual thraldom; and that therefore we are bound to take him for our God alone, and to keep all his commandments.[4]

We find here a cohesive, consistent understanding of the nature of the believer's obedience in every epoch of the covenant of grace. In this regard, the authors of the *Kerux* review carefully explain the significance of WLC 101.

2. WCF 7.5.
3. Ibid., 7.6.
4. WLC 101.

> A direct line is drawn between his covenantal relation-
> ship with Israel under Moses and his covenantal relation
> with all his people at every other time. Furthermore, the
> essentially gracious nature of that covenant relation is
> further underscored in terms of Exodus-typology: "... as
> he brought them [Israel] out of their bondage in Egypt,
> so he delivers us from our spiritual thralldom." Finally,
> the essential identity of the conditions or obligations of
> that covenant is also highlighted: "and that therefore we
> are bound to take him for our God alone, and to keep
> all his commandments." . . . The confession is clear: the
> covenant made with Israel in the Decalogue declares the
> same salvation and imposes the same obligation to obe-
> dience as those in the new covenant.[5]

The obedience required under Moses is viewed in light of the
deliverance of the Exodus. The obedience of the believer in the
New Covenant is likewise understood in light of the greater deliverance by Christ from our sinful condition. Therefore, the Larger
Catechism introduces its exposition of the Ten Commandments
by positioning them squarely within the redemptive context of the
one covenant of grace. The obligations imposed upon Israel in the
Ten Commandments do not function in any way as a covenant
of works in which their obedience would merit blessing. Rather,
it functions solely as a rule of life informing them of the proper
expression of their faith—reverent, thankful obedience for God's
gracious redemption.

This gracious function of the law as a rule of life is set forth
and explained further in the first part of WCF 19.6.

> Although true believers be not under the law, as a cov-
> enant of works, to be thereby justified, or condemned;
> yet is it of great use to them, as well as to others; in that,
> as a rule of life informing them of the will of God, and
> their duty, it directs and binds them to walk accordingly;
> discovering also the sinful pollutions of their nature,
> hearts, and lives; so as, examining themselves thereby,
> they may come to further conviction of, humiliation for,

---

5. Dennison et al., review of *TLNF*, 83.

and hatred against sin, together with a clearer sight of
the need they have of Christ, and the perfection of his
obedience.

In the covenant of grace, for those who are justified by
faith (see Gen 15:6; Rom 4), the law is a rule of life, which aids
in sanctification, for it continues to be a manifestation of God's
perfect righteousness. Whether in the Old Testament or the New
Testament, the law serves the redeemed people of God by showing
them the seriousness of their sin as well as "a clearer sight of the
need they have of Christ, and the perfection of his obedience."[6]
Our Standards make clear that believers (Old and New Testament
alike) cannot use the law as a covenant of works.[7]

Blessings and Curses of the Law in the Mosaic Covenant

It is at this point that an important question is often raised: "What
about the blessings and curses listed in such passages as Leviticus
26 and Deuteronomy 28?" It would seem that the presence of these
sanctions within the Mosaic covenant undercut the idea that this
administration of the covenant is purely gracious in character.
How can we avoid the implication that these blessings and curses
are the evidence of a works-principle? It is often claimed that Israel either merited blessing or cursing based on their obedience or
disobedience to the Mosaic law. Yet, the Confession also addresses
this issue and provides an explanation that is in keeping with the
doctrine of the unity of the covenant of grace, as well as the gracious function of the law. The second half of WCF 19.6 maintains
that the law (even when viewed in light of its blessings and curses)
is still functioning as "a rule of life" for believers rather than as a
"covenant of works."

---

6. WCF 19.6.

7. See Venema's explanation of WCF 19.6, in which he remarks: "As a matter of fact, the Confession expressly denies that the law was given through
Moses 'as a covenant of works'" (review of *TLNF*, 75).

It is likewise of use to the regenerate, to restrain their corruptions, in that it forbids sin: and the threatenings of it serve to show what even their sins deserve; and what afflictions, in this life, they may expect for them, although freed from the curse thereof threatened in the law. The promises of it, in like manner, show them God's approbation of obedience, and what blessings they may expect upon the performance thereof: although not as due to them by the law as a covenant of works. So as, a man's doing good, and refraining from evil, because the law encourageth to the one, and deterreth from the other, is no evidence of his being under the law; and, not under grace.

Patrick Ramsey provides helpful commentary on this matter concerning the blessings and curses within the covenant of grace.

According to this section of the Confession, the curses ("threatenings") of the Mosaic Law teach the regenerate what temporal afflictions they may expect when they sin while the blessings ("promises") instruct them concerning the benefits they may expect when they obey. Saving faith "trembles" at these curses and "embraces" the blessings for "this life, and that which is to come."

To establish a connection between obedience and blessing and disobedience and cursing is for many—notably antinomians—to establish in some sense a covenant of works. The divines were certainly aware of this possible misunderstanding. After all, they debated this issue for years. Consequently, they made it explicitly clear that such a connection does not in any form or fashion indicate that man is under a covenant of works.[8]

WCF 19 makes it clear that the blessings and curses are a part of the law's function as a rule of life—as it declares to believers the approval of their obedience as well as the seriousness of what their sins deserve. The Confession is explicit: the blessings and the curses of the law in the Mosaic covenant do not function in any way as a covenant of works. As the Confession indicates so

8. Ramsey, "In Defense of Moses," 14–15.

clearly in its conclusion of this section, this paradigm of blessings and threatenings within the Mosaic covenant "is no evidence of [a believer's] being under the law; and, not under grace."[9]

THE NATURE OF THE MOSAIC COVENANT IN THE REPUBLICATION PARADIGM

How does the Republication Paradigm line up with the teaching of the Confession regarding the unity of the covenant of grace? Earlier we indicated how the Republication Paradigm divides the Mosaic covenant into two distinct levels. There is a lower-foundational level of grace, and there is a meritorious works-principle operating at a temporal, upper-typological level. Due to the lower-foundational level, which applies to eternal salvation, the authors of *TLNF* seek to affirm their agreement with the Confession's understanding that the Mosaic covenant is part of the covenant of grace.

> I hope you didn't understand me to mean that the Mosaic covenant is a covenant of works; I believe that it is an administration of the covenant of grace, but that there is this principle of works operative at a typological level as part of this administration.[10]

> In other words, in some sense, the covenant of works was republished at Sinai. It was not republished, however, as the covenant of works per se, but as part of the covenant of grace, which pointed to the person and the work of Christ.[11]

How do these affirmations apply to the nature of the Mosaic covenant on the upper-typological level? Are the essential elements of the covenant of grace (the condition of faith; the reward of eternal life) consistently maintained in the Republication Paradigm?

9. WCF 19.6.
10. *TLNF*, 3.
11. Ibid., 11.

This is where things become complicated. Despite its affirmation that the Mosaic covenant is "part of the covenant of grace," the republication formulation of this covenant includes elements that differ in substance from the covenant of grace. In the Republication Paradigm, the Mosaic covenant includes a different set of essential elements on the typological level—the condition of meritorious works in order to earn the reward of temporal life in the promised land. Furthermore, in the Republication Paradigm's formulation, the character or nature of the Mosaic covenant as a whole seems to be determined by this upper-typological level. The Mosaic administration is typically contrasted with the nature of the Abrahamic and New covenant administrations. This seems to imply that the nature or substance of the Mosaic covenant differs in some degree from other administrations of the covenant of grace. The following quotes illustrate our point.

> The Old Covenant was a breakable covenant, it was made obsolete; indeed, the promises in the Abrahamic covenant entailed that the old covenant would pass away: it was a planned obsolescence.[12]

> Although the substance of the covenant of grace is the same in both testaments, in the old covenant there was the need for compliance so that this would be the meritorious grounds for Israel's continuation in the land, the typological kingdom . . . God does not call the New Testament church to obedience in exactly the same way as he did the Old Testament saints in the Sinaitic covenant or for the same purpose, and neither should we: the promise of tenure in the land is over . . . Therefore, the new covenant context has essentially changed matters here. The new context of Christ having come has changed matters.[13]

12. Estelle, "Leviticus 18:5," 130.
13. Ibid., 136.

> The Abrahamic Covenant is Characterized by Faith; the Sinai Covenant is Characterized by Works of the Law.[14]

> The consistent use of the synecdoche "promise" to refer to the Abrahamic administration, and the equally consistent use of the synecdoche "law" to refer to the Sinai administration, demonstrate convincingly that Paul did not conceive these two covenants as similar in kind, but rather as dissimilar in kind: one is characteristically promissory; the other is characteristically legal.[15]

> What we must not do is evade the plain teaching of Paul that the Sinai covenant itself, as it was delivered by the hand of Moses 430 years after the Abrahamic Covenant, was a different covenant, different in kind, characteristically legal, Gentile-excluding, non-justifying because it was characterized by works, and therefore cursing its recipients and bearing children for slavery.[16]

> Granted, the Mosaic Covenant in its typological priestly embodiment of mediation (the ceremonial law) must be viewed as an administration of the covenant of grace. Nevertheless, the Mosaic Law more narrowly considered embodies what can only be described best as a works principle. This is what others and I mean by "republication" of the covenant of works in Moses.[17]

What do these quotes demonstrate? They show how the Mosaic covenant is characterized as a "law covenant" in contrast to the gracious nature of the Abrahamic and New covenants in the Republication Paradigm. This is why the quotes above raise so many questions of concern. How can the Mosaic covenant and Abrahamic covenant be *in essence* covenants of grace when one is described as unbreakable and the other breakable?[18] How can they

---

14. Gordon, "Abraham and Sinai Contrasted," 246.

15. Ibid., 250.

16. Ibid., 251.

17. Baugh, "Galatians 5:1–6," 260.

18. Estelle, "Leviticus 18:5," 130.

be described as "different covenants" which are "different in kind" and at the same time be covenants of grace?[19] How can the Abrahamic and Sinaitic covenants be characterized by diametrically opposite principles of faith and works, and both still be *essentially* the same covenant?

This characterization of the Mosaic covenant within the Republication Paradigm seems to depart from the teaching of the Westminster Standards. In our consideration of WCF 19 above, the believer's relationship to the moral law as a rule of life necessitates that the Mosaic covenant be understood as a covenant of grace in *substance*, as opposed to a covenant of works. The Standards are consistent in maintaining the gracious character and nature of the covenant of grace in every epoch, which, by definition, excludes any element of meritorious obedience. At best, it is very unclear as to how the Republication Paradigm can maintain a theologically consistent view of the nature of the Mosaic covenant—one that harmonizes with the nature and substance of the covenant of grace, as well as the teaching of the Westminster Standards.

THE UNSTABLE RESULTS OF THE REPUBLICATION PARADIGM

It has become evident that two different systems of interpretation are at odds with one another. As we discuss the theological instability of the Republication Paradigm with respect to the nature of the Mosaic covenant within the covenant of grace, we will focus our analysis on three key points.

1. The mixture of essential elements from two different covenants in the Mosaic covenant.

2. The lack of a clear distinction between a covenant of works and a covenant of grace.

3. The doctrine of justification depends on clear covenantal definitions.

19. Gordon, "Abraham and Sinai Contrasted," 250–51.

1. The Mixture of Essential Elements from Two Different Covenants

We have attempted to demonstrate the clear differences between the formulation of the Mosaic covenant which is presented in the Republication Paradigm from the one we find within the Westminster Standards. Serious theological problems arise when one attempts to combine or mix essential or constituent parts of substantially different covenants. According to the paradigm of the Standards, it is impossible to argue that a single covenant contains two essentially different sets of conditions and rewards. Yet, the Republication Paradigm affirms that on the temporal, upper-typological level of the Mosaic covenant there is one set of essential elements: (1) the requirement or condition of imperfect, sincere obedience; and (2) the promise or reward of temporal life, granted on the basis of merit. On the gracious, lower-foundational level there is another set of essential elements that belong to the covenant of grace: (1) the condition of faith; and (2) the promise of eternal life. In this view, these essential or constituent elements of the upper-typological level of the Mosaic covenant stand in opposition to the constituent elements of the covenant of grace, to which it is said to belong. This combination or mixture of the essential parts of two different covenants is confusing, and is a clear departure from the confessional conception of the Mosaic covenant as a pure covenant of grace in its substance and essential parts.

Furthermore, this combination of substantially differing elements in the construction of the two levels of the Mosaic covenant necessarily leads to the creation of two competing "natures" within a single covenant. One nature must certainly give way to the other. It is clear from the above quotes from *TLNF* (in the previous section) that the Mosaic covenant is characterized as a "legal" covenant which is "dissimilar in kind" from the "promissory" Abrahamic covenant.[20] The Abrahamic covenant "is characterized by faith" but the Mosaic covenant "is characterized by works of the

---

20. Gordon, "Abraham and Sinai Contrasted," 250.

law."[21] It would seem that due emphasis on the gracious nature of the Mosaic covenant (as expressed in classic Reformed theology) has given way to the radical characterization of the Sinai administration as a "non-justifying" covenant of works.[22] Thus, in the Republication Paradigm, the "dual nature" of the Mosaic covenant has led to the creation of an incoherent, unstable system. Grace and works have been combined as opposing principles in a single covenant in a "tug of war" kind of tension with one another.

2. No Clear Distinction between a Covenant of Works and a Covenant of Grace

The previous point leads us to ask a specific question: "Since the Mosaic covenant in the Republication Paradigm possesses a dual nature, is the Mosaic covenant in fact a covenant of grace or a covenant of works?" It is difficult, if not impossible, to be certain. The presence of the two levels of grace and works, has led to something of an identity crisis for the Mosaic covenant in the Republication Paradigm. In comparing and contrasting the two levels of the Mosaic covenant, with their respective sets of differing *essential elements*, it is very difficult to clearly identify the Mosaic covenant as an administration of the covenant of grace.

For that matter, it is also difficult to identify the Mosaic covenant as a covenant of works. Given all the legal language that is used in *TLNF* to characterize the Mosaic covenant ("breakable," "meritorious," "works of the law," "works principle," "characteristically legal," etc.), one would expect the upper-typological level to possess a clear "covenant of works" nature, in and of itself. However, this is not the case. Even when considered apart from its association with the lower-foundational level of grace (in the Republication Paradigm), the temporal, typological level cannot clearly be identified in terms of a purely meritorious works arrangement.

---

21. Ibid., 246.
22. Ibid., 251.

In the Confession, God's favorable acceptance of imperfect, relative obedience indicates and requires the presence of pure grace and faith in the Mediator of the covenant of grace. If man's obedience falls "short of the glory of God," how can he approve it as acceptable in his sight by a principle of merit in contrast to grace? According to our understanding of God's character and the nature of sin, the bestowal of favor in the face of demerit requires grace. This critique equally applies to the upper-typological level of the Republication Paradigm as well as to the lower-foundational level. Why then refer to the Mosaic covenant as the republication of the covenant of works? As Mark Jones writes:

> The WCF clearly speaks of the prelapsarian covenant of works as demanding "perfect and personal obedience" (7.2; 19.1; WLC 20; WSC 12). Does it not follow that any covenant that does not require both "perfect and personal obedience" is not a covenant of works, even at the typological level? But, in two places (137, 301) we are informed that the obedience required in the Mosaic covenant was "imperfect/sincere obedience." The WCF shows that the only covenant in which God accepts imperfect obedience is the covenant of grace (WCF 16.6). To say, then, that the Mosaic covenant is in some sense a covenant of works can be especially misleading to the average reader in light of the aforementioned concern.[23]

In contrast to the Confession, the Republication Paradigm is no longer able to clearly distinguish between a covenant of works and a covenant of grace. Not only is the republication formulation of the Mosaic covenant "especially misleading" in its use of the labels "covenant of works" as well as "covenant of grace" (according to established confessional categories), we believe that the inability to clearly delineate a pure works covenant from a pure grace covenant may also adversely impact the doctrine of justification.

---

23. Jones, review of *TLNF*, 119.

3. Justification Depends on Clear Covenantal Definitions

The clear distinction between the covenant of works and the covenant of grace in the Confession provides a stable foundation for the doctrine of justification. Justification by grace has meaning in the context of the covenant of grace only as it is contrasted with justification by works. Yet, the Republication Paradigm has introduced a type of justification by works in the life of the nation of Israel in the Mosaic covenant (on the upper-typological level) while simultaneously affirming the impossibility of justification by works (on the lower-foundational level). The opposite principles at work on these two levels would traditionally demand the existence of two separate covenants, by definition. In our view, the failure to clearly distinguish a covenant of works from a covenant of grace is in danger of blurring the respective elements of each covenant within a single covenantal arrangement. This pitfall appears to be a very real possibility in the Republication Paradigm.

If the distinction between grace and works is blurred in one part of the system, it would logically follow that the distinction will be blurred in another part of the system. This is especially the case when the blurring occurs in the definition of a covenant of works. It has been shown in part 1 that Norman Shepherd blurred works and grace in the covenant of works, which undermined the doctrine of justification by denying the imputation of the active obedience of Christ. He did this by reformulating the works arrangement with Adam into one of pure grace. The Republication Paradigm commits the same error on the opposite end by reformulating an essentially gracious arrangement with Israel into one that includes meritorious works. The presence of a works-merit principle for receiving God's favor cannot coexist (by definition) in a covenant that is based on the necessity of God's grace for fallen sinners. The doctrine of justification depends on the clear separation of works and grace by way of clear covenantal definitions. Thus, if the Republication Paradigm blurs the distinction between works and grace in its formulation of the Mosaic covenant in the covenant of grace, it is difficult to see (as in the case of Shepherd) how the result of inherent theological instability in the doctrine of justification can ultimately be avoided. This resultant instability will be developed in more detail in the following two chapters.

11

The Doctrines of Merit and Justice and the Republication Paradigm

THE DOCTRINES OF MERIT AND JUSTICE IN THE WESTMINSTER STANDARDS

The Westminster Standards maintain a direct connection between the doctrine of merit and the doctrine of God's justice. The reason for the connection is clear. God's justice determines the nature of merit. God's own character defines and delimits what he accepts as meritorious. When we talk about merit, we must begin by talking about God. God's attribute of justice looms large in the Bible and in our Standards.[1] This attribute refers to the fact that God's nature is in itself holy and just. God's perfect justice involves the necessity within God's nature to give to each one his due. Man is a moral creature who is accountable to his Creator for what he does. God's justice requires a full accountability of man to himself; his own nature sets the standard of justice and judgment. This involves that which is referred to in theology as God's *distributive* justice. In other words, it involves God's distribution of rewards or pun-

1. WSC 4; WLC 7; WCF 2.1–2.

ishments to man. In Reformed theology, God's distributive justice requires that a merited reward ("properly" or "strictly" speaking) be absolutely perfect. By necessity of his just and holy nature, as the Confession states, God is a being who is "most just and terrible in his judgments, hating all sin, and who will by no means clear the guilty."[2]

In light of God's attribute of justice, the criteria for a meritorious work may be defined. In part 2 (chap. 6), we outlined five necessary conditions in the definition of a truly and properly meritorious work. For the purposes of our present discussion, we may boil these down to two key conditions. For a work to be truly and properly meritorious, it must: (1) be absolutely perfect; and (2) be performed by one who is ontologically equal with God (i.e., infinite, eternal, and unchangeable in his being). Adam could satisfy the first condition, as he was created in original righteousness. But only Jesus Christ could satisfy the second, since he is both true man and true God, being the same in substance and equal with the Father. This lays the groundwork for the important distinction between Christ's *strict* merit and Adam's *covenant* merit, which was discussed earlier (see part 2, chap. 6).

The Unique Merit of the Second Adam

Here, it is important to underscore how the uniqueness of Christ's merit plays a significant role in our understanding of merit and justice. Our understanding of merit is derived from the standard of God's justice. When we begin with God's being and character, we are able to see the uniqueness of Christ's meritorious work in connection with the uniqueness of his person. Our Larger Catechism makes this connection clear.

> It was requisite that the mediator should be God, that he might sustain and keep the human nature from sinking under the infinite wrath of God, and the power of death; give worth and efficacy to his sufferings, obedience, and

2. WCF 2.1.

> intercession; and to satisfy God's justice, procure his favor, purchase a peculiar people, give his Spirit to them, conquer all their enemies, and bring them to everlasting salvation.[3]

Note how the merits of his active and passive obedience require that the mediator must truly be God. The value of his merit is rooted in his divine nature, and is thus determined ontologically.

The confessions and creeds of the Reformed churches will not allow us to take for granted the uniqueness and necessity of Christ's person and work. This is because merit is connected to and defined by ontology (i.e., God's being and attributes). The Heidelberg Catechism particularly highlights the necessity of Christ's infinite, divine nature in his satisfaction of sin through his obedience and death. Lord's Day 5 of the Heidelberg begins its discussion of our deliverance by emphasizing the necessity of satisfaction: "God requires that his justice be satisfied. Therefore the claims of his justice must be paid in full, either by ourselves or another."[4] It is clear that neither we ourselves nor any mere creature (however sinless) could bear the weight of God's infinite wrath against sin. The only sufficient satisfaction for sin must be offered by one who is both "truly human and truly righteous" and also "true God."[5] Lord's Day 6 goes on to explain that Christ must be true man because "God's justice demands that human nature, which has sinned, must pay for its sin."[6] He must be true God "so that, by the power of his divinity, he might bear the weight of God's anger in his humanity and earn for us and restore to us righteousness and life."[7]

It is abundantly clear in these creeds that the traditional paradigm has defined "merit" in such a way as to highlight the singular glory of Christ in his active and passive obedience for our salvation. Christ obeyed where the first man failed, thus performing perfect, personal obedience to the law, and fully satisfying the

3. WLC 38.
4. Heidelberg Catechism 12.
5. Ibid., 15.
6. Ibid., 16.
7. Ibid., 17.

first condition of merit. Because he is God, Christ's person is of infinite value. His obedience and sacrifice carries an infinite inherent dignity and value. Christ alone can satisfy the *second condition* of merit as he is ontologically equal with his Father. Thus, as the God-man, Jesus Christ alone is capable of fully meeting the bar of God's justice so as to "strictly" or "properly" merit eternal life.

The Lesser Merit of the First Adam

Adam's obedience would only have been meritorious by means of "covenant merit"—not the "strict merit" attained by Christ. Adam serves merely as a type of Christ (Rom 5:14). In Adam's case, there was a need for voluntary condescension because "the distance between God and the creature is so great."[8] The Confession begins building its covenant theology here in chapter 7 on the foundation stone of section one. Although condescension is necessary in the establishment of the covenant of works with Adam, we may still speak of a form of human merit that stands in contrast to redemptive grace. Nevertheless, the possibility of meriting the reward of eternal life rests upon the fulfillment of a particular kind of condition. Adam's "covenant merit" is still related to God's being and nature. God will not compromise his justice during the time of Adam's probation in Eden. Adam can only pass his probation and merit the reward of eternal life on the basis of perfect, personal, and perpetual obedience to God's law.[9] What is clear in God's requirement for Adam, a mere creature, is that anything less than the kind of obedience that accords with God's righteousness and the standards of his justice (again, 1 above), would simply not qualify as being adequate to merit *any* reward. In fact, less than exact and entire obedience will only merit God's eternal wrath. God's justice demands it.

8. WCF 7.1.
9. Ibid., 7.2; 19.1.

The Absence of Merit in Every Son of Adam

The same standards for merit and divine justice remain intact after the fall. Just as the requirement for Adam's obedience before the fall was in keeping with God's own attribute of justice, so also, the bar of his righteousness is unchanging. The moral law is an abiding manifestation of God's own attribute of righteousness and an expression of his own holy character. Sin is always defined as a deviation from God's law. In order for any human work to merit any kind of reward or blessing from the God of the Bible, it must be perfect and without sin. God is infinite, eternal, and unchangeable in his holiness and justice.[10] Any sinful defect or imperfection in man must necessarily disqualify him from the possibility of meriting God's blessing or favor. How could it be any other way? According to his very own nature and character, God would be unjust to accept and reward such works. It is a contradiction for God to reward an inherently demeritorious work as if it were meritorious.

God's Grace and Christ's Glory

The story of the Bible is all about God's grace after the fall. That is why Augustine asserted against Pelagius and the Pelagians the complete and total inability of sinners to merit *anything* in the sight of God.

> Here let human merits, which have perished through Adam, keep silence, and let that grace of God reign which reigns through Jesus Christ our Lord, the only Son of God.[11]

We must trumpet God's grace "which reigns through Jesus Christ our Lord, the only Son of God." As was demonstrated in part 2, this Augustinian paradigm is assumed and taught in the Westminster Standards. If man in his state of innocence is unable to offer an obedience that truly fulfills the essential conditions of

---

10. WSC 4.

11. Augustine, *On the Predestination of the Saints*, 15.31, 5:513.

merit (properly speaking) according to God's justice, how much less in his state of sin! No sinner or group of sinners, however obedient and sincere, could ever offer an obedience that God reckons as meritorious in *any sense* of the word. Thus, in the traditional paradigm, Christ's merits magnify the singular glory of the infinite value of his person and perfection of his work. The Lord Jesus is in a class by himself. Everyone else: Adam and his sinful posterity—not to mention the sinless angels—shall fall on their knees before his throne, crying, "Holy, Holy, Holy!"

Merit in the Traditional Paradigm

Strict Merit	Covenant Merit	No Merit
⬇	⬇	⬇
Christ	**Adam**	**Israel**
Perfect Obedience of Son of God	Perfect Obedience of Creature	Imperfect Obedience of Fallen Creatures

The Redefinition of Merit in the Republication Paradigm

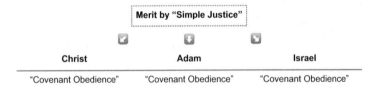

	Merit by "Simple Justice"	
⬇	⬇	⬇
Christ	**Adam**	**Israel**
"Covenant Obedience"	"Covenant Obedience"	"Covenant Obedience"

THE REDEFINITION OF MERIT AND JUSTICE IN THE REPUBLICATION PARADIGM

In part 2, we outlined how the Republication Paradigm alters the traditional definitions of both justice and merit. Here we would like to review how this redefinition takes place.

Ontological Equality Irrelevant

The Republication Paradigm rejects the idea that Adam's reward in the covenant of works would only have been meritorious because of God's voluntary condescension. It rejects the idea that the ontological inequality between God and man should play any role in determining the nature of Adam's merit. Kline viewed Adam's creation in the image of God *as* a covenantal event. Rather than viewing the establishment of the covenant of works as a distinct act of God's providence after creation (as in WSC 12), it is viewed as being coextensive with the very act of creation. As VanDrunen states: "God's creating Adam in his image and the establishment of the covenant are aspects of the same act."[12] The Republication Paradigm thus conflates the distinct acts of creation and covenant-making into a single event which no longer requires the doctrine of God's voluntary condescension (as taught in WCF 7.1).

How does this affect the traditional view of merit? Above we noted that the traditional viewpoint required two essential conditions for a work to be meritorious: (1) moral perfection: and (2) ontological equality. The Republication Paradigm's redefinition of the covenant, which excludes the idea of voluntary condescension, eliminates the need for the second condition (ontological equality) in the definition of merit. The reality of the "infinite distance that is between us and God"[13] becomes irrelevant to the definition of merit. This paradigm excludes altogether the consideration of the ontological disproportion between the Creator and creature in its *definition* of merit. Note the difference between this redefinition and the traditional paradigm. Instead of a "covenant merit" which stood over against Christ's "strict merit," we are left with only one category of merit. The Republication Paradigm, especially as it is articulated by Kline, *defines* "merit" by the principle of "simple justice."

Moral Perfection Unnecessary

How does the republication view of "simple justice" affect the traditional understanding of merit? Kline's redefinition of merit not

---

12. VanDrunen, "Natural Law," 291.

13. WCF 16.5.

only excluded voluntary condescension, but also defined merit solely in terms of the will of God as expressed in the covenant. In other words, "simple justice" teaches that the "merit" required of Adam (or anyone else) was simply *whatever God said it would be.* If one fulfills the stipulation of a given covenant, then God is "just" to reward the obedience as "meritorious." A failure to reward such obedience would be considered "unjust." The implication is that God's nature, which is infinite in being and most just, no longer plays a determinative role in the *definition* of justice as it does in the traditional paradigm. This alteration has repercussions beyond the situation with Adam in the garden.

Note the clear difference between Kline's "simple justice" and the traditional paradigm: It is no longer necessary for the work to be perfect in order to be properly meritorious before God. In other words, Kline's redefinition of merit constituted a rejection of both of the essential conditions of merit as defined in the traditional view (1 and 2 above—i.e., moral perfection and ontological equality). Such considerations are irrelevant and unnecessary in the Republication Paradigm. Thus, God could (theoretically) accept an obedience as meritorious that was quite different in quality from the perfection required of Adam or Christ. Even more importantly, he could accept as meritorious an imperfect, sin-tainted obedience that stands opposed to the inherent holiness of his own nature. In this paradigm, the single category of merit applies equally to Christ, Adam, and Israel.

Merit Possible for Fallen Man

What was absolutely impossible after the fall in the traditional paradigm is now a real possibility. Merit has been redefined in such a way that an *imperfect* obedience (vs. moral perfection) could be constituted by God as the meritorious ground for rewarding *fallen sinners* (vs. sinless Adam's *covenant merit* and Christ's *strict merit*). This is precisely what has happened in the Republication Paradigm's conception of the typological works principle in post-fall history. Israel is said to be under a works-merit probation in which God would be obligated to reward sin-tainted obedience on the basis of merit. In addition to Israel, biblical figures such as Noah, Abraham, and David, are said to be under a typological merit paradigm in which their acts of obedience under the terms of God's covenant arrangement were truly meritorious. As evidence of this, we would direct the reader to the writings of Kline, Estelle, Horton, and Johnson, which were referenced earlier.[14]

THE UNSTABLE RESULTS OF THE REPUBLICATION PARADIGM

In view of the previous two sections (and part 2), it is clear that the Republication Paradigm has redefined the historical and traditional category of merit and its relationship to God's justice. This can result in theological instability in the rest of the Reformed system. As we discuss the instability of the Republication Paradigm with respect to the doctrines of merit and justice, we will focus our analysis on three key points.

1. The necessity of Christ's perfect active obedience for our justification.

2. The necessity of Christ's divine nature in his satisfaction for sin.

3. The singular glory of Christ's meritorious obedience as Mediator of the covenant of grace.

1. The Necessity of Christ's Perfect Active Obedience

In the Republication Paradigm, the redefinition of merit and justice has compromised the foundation of the necessity of Christ's perfect active obedience for our justification. It is commonly understood that Christ had to succeed where the first Adam failed. This requires Christ to perform personal, perfect, and perpetual obedience. This active obedience is an essential component in the

14. See chap. 5; see also appendix 1.

righteousness imputed to us in our justification, granting us the right and the title of eternal life. These points are not under dispute. The problem arises when we consider the reason why perfect obedience is *necessary*. Why do the Reformed creeds teach that Christ's active obedience *must* be perfect for our justification?

In the traditional paradigm, the reason for Christ's perfect obedience is found in the necessity of what God's attributes require. According to our view of God's attribute of infinite justice, it seems incomprehensible that God's just nature could ever allow him to reward a demeritorious work as if it were meritorious. This ontological "freedom" given to God in the Republication Paradigm would seem to allow God to contradict himself. What do we mean by this?

In the Republication Paradigm, God's "simple justice" does not require Christ's obedience to be perfect *by definition*. Simple justice would instruct Israel to consider their sin-tainted works as meritorious and deserving of reward on the basis of God's covenant Word. Someone may ask the Israelite under the Republication Paradigm, "How can you, a sinful creature, perform imperfect, sin-tainted works that are meritorious? How are they deserving of blessing from a perfectly holy and righteous God?" The answer would be, "According to 'simple justice.' It doesn't matter that my works are tainted with sin. God did not require perfection in the covenant he made at Sinai for me to merit temporal blessings and retain my life in the promised land. I have simply obeyed God's covenant stipulations (albeit, imperfectly), and now—according to 'simple justice'—he owes me the reward that he promised."

In light of the concept of "simple justice," it is very difficult to see how the Republication Paradigm helps Israel discern the necessity of someone else performing perfect obedience to merit a reward on their behalf. If their imperfect obedience can be constituted as the meritorious ground of reward, where then do we find the ground for the *necessity* of the absolute perfect obedience of Christ to merit our salvation? By redefining the traditional view of merit, the Republication Paradigm has actually destroyed a significant portion of the traditional theological basis for the necessity of Christ's perfect, active obedience.

In the traditional paradigm, the *definition* of justice and merit *absolutely necessitates* the perfect obedience of Christ to merit our salvation. In the Republication Paradigm, the *definition* of justice and merit no longer requires moral perfection. According to this system, Israel is able to truly merit blessing through an obedience that is only relative and imperfect (i.e., sinful). This revised definition of merit no longer absolutely requires perfection to meet the bar of God's justice, either for Adam, for Israel, or for Christ.

2. The Necessity of Christ's Divine Nature

In the Republication Paradigm, the theological foundation for the necessity of Christ's divine nature in his satisfaction for sin is compromised. We have seen how the traditional paradigm includes the *absolute necessity* of Christ's divine nature in order to perform his work of redemption. The mediator had to be God in order to pay an infinite debt incurred by sin. Sin, as well as righteousness, is understood ontologically—in relationship to God's infinite nature. Since man's transgression is against an infinitely just and holy God, sin makes man necessarily subject to an infinitely just penalty— the eternal fire of hell.

In the Republication Paradigm, righteousness and justice have been redefined in terms of the simple fulfillment of the covenant stipulations ("simple justice"). Ontological considerations have been removed from the *definitions* of merit and justice. The infinite, eternal character of God's being no longer play any role in our understanding of justice, merit, or (by implication) sin. If this is the case, it is difficult to see what basis there is for insisting on the *necessity* of Christ's divine nature in his satisfaction for sin. If God is free to "covenantally" define merit in such a way that Adam's finite obedience could be truly worthy of an infinite reward, what *absolute need* is there for Christ to be truly God? Even more pointedly, if God is free to accept the sinful obedience of Noah, Abraham, and Israel as truly the meritorious grounds of reward, why is there an *absolute need* for Christ's perfect obedience? Could not God have simply given us a Messiah who was a mere man, and covenantally stipulated that he simply perform a few acts of obedience and then die in some other way? If God's covenant Word *defines* what is just, what is to stop God from making another arrangement than the one he has made with Christ for the salvation of sinners? The Republication Paradigm clearly affirms that Christ is God and that his obedience was perfect. The problem lies in the fact that their *redefinition* of justice and merit has removed the traditional basis for their affirmation of an *absolute necessity* in Christ's satisfaction and our justification.

3. The Singular Glory of Christ's Meritorious Obedience

In the Republication Paradigm, the redefinition of merit and justice serves to undermine the singular glory of Christ's meritorious obedience. Historically, only sinless Adam and sinless Christ can merit. There are only two Adam figures in the history of redemption. In the traditional paradigm, Christ's meritorious obedience is in a category of its own. Adam's merit was merely "covenant merit" which required the voluntary condescension of God to constitute it as such. The republication formulation of Israel's merit as a "corporate Adam" is wholly non-existent. The traditional, Augustinian paradigm will not allow a group of fallen sinners to merit anything as a "corporate Adam," nor does it allow God to even theoretically put them under a merit-based probation. Christ's merit stands alone. Unlike Israel's so-called "merit" (in the Republication Paradigm), Christ's obedience is utterly flawless. Unlike Adam's "covenant merit," Christ's merit requires no voluntary condescension. It is intrinsically worthy of the reward of eternal life and more than sufficient to pay the infinite debt incurred by sin.

In the Republication Paradigm, the redefinition of merit and justice is simply unable to magnify the unparalleled glory of Christ's obedience. What do we mean? Merit has been reduced to only one category (determined by "simple justice") common to Adam, Israel, and Christ. We now have three "Adams" instead of two. National Israel is treated as a "third Adam" as her "meritori-ous" works are viewed as a reenactment of the first Adam's and a preview of the last Adam's works. Although those who hold the republication view acknowledge that the nature and character of obedience differs in each case, merit has been *defined* so broadly as to properly include each as *truly meritorious*. Christ is no longer in a category of his own. Rather than exalting the unique glory of Christ's obedience, this redefinition of merit brings Christ down to the level of Adam, a mere creature, and—what is worse—to that of fallen and depraved sinners. According to this *redefinition* of merit, these figures are interchangeable—for each can equally perform meritorious works according to "simple justice." Clearly, proponents of the republication position affirm that Christ alone can merit salvation and that his obedience alone is perfect. How-ever, these differences between the merit of Christ and that of Noah, Abraham, or Israel are not accounted for in their *definition* of merit. Proponents of the republication view sincerely desire to exalt the glory of Christ and the perfection of his obedience. In our estimation, further consideration of the implications of their redefinition of merit is needed in these areas. By *defining* merit in a way that applies equally to Adam, fallen sinners, and Christ, the Republication Paradigm fails to consistently exalt the singular glory of the God-man, Jesus Christ.

12

The Doctrine of Good Works and the Republication Paradigm

THE DOCTRINE OF GOOD WORKS IN THE WESTMINSTER STANDARDS

Closely related to the previous discussion of merit and justice is the Reformed doctrine of good works. Our Standards draw a clear distinction between the two covenants—of Works and of Grace— and their respective ways for man's works to be accepted and rewarded by God. The *first* way is by means of perfect and personal obedience in the covenant of works. The *second* is by means of sincere, yet imperfect obedience in the covenant of grace—on the basis of the imputed righteousness of another.

God's Acceptance and Reward of Obedience in the Covenant of Works

The *first* way in which man's works might be accepted and rewarded is by means of merit in the covenant of works. In this arrangement, Adam's obedience would serve as the meritorious ground (through God's voluntary condescension) of the reward. As was discussed previously, not just any kind of obedience would meet God's requirement. Adam's obedience was to be *perfect* and *personal*. Adam's obedience had to be *perfect* in order to conform to the divine standard of God's righteousness. Since Adam was created without sin in the image of God, in true righteousness and holiness, he possessed the natural ability to perform this perfect obedience.

Adam's obedience also was required to be *personal*—he himself had to perform these works. He could not receive help or assistance from anyone else. No other obedience or righteousness could be credited to his account. The covenant of works arrangement entailed that Adam would either stand or fall as the covenant head who must personally obey the required stipulation. Although voluntary condescension was necessary for the establishment of the covenant and its terms,[1] the promised reward of life would be obtained by Adam's *perfect* and *personal* works, in contrast to grace.

God's Acceptance and Reward of Obedience in the Covenant of Grace

The *second* way that man's works might be accepted and rewarded by God is through the covenant of grace. The *nature* of these works and the *basis* of their reward is quite different than what we find in the covenant of works.

The covenant of works required perfection in order to merit a reward. By contrast, our Confession of Faith teaches that there can be no meritorious works in the covenant of grace.[2] This is due to the fact that even the believer's best works are far from perfect. Instead, by sheer grace, God "is pleased to accept and to reward that which is sincere, although accompanied by many weaknesses

---

1. See WCF 7.1.
2. See ibid., chap. 16, "Of Good Works."

and imperfections."[3] The implication is clear. The acceptance and reward of *sincere*, yet *imperfect* obedience by God is a sure sign of a covenant of pure grace, in distinction from a covenant of works arrangement.

How then is God able to accept and reward imperfect obedience while his righteous nature inherently demands perfection? The reason can *never* be that God lowers the standard of his perfect justice in the covenant of grace in order to count imperfect works as meritorious. Instead, the Confession answers this question by grounding God's acceptance of the believer's imperfect *works* in the Lord's acceptance of the believer's *person* in justification.

> Notwithstanding, the persons of believers being accepted through Christ, their good works also are accepted in him; not as though they were in this life wholly unblamable and unreprovable in God's sight; but that he, looking upon them in his Son, is pleased to accept and reward that which is sincere, although accompanied with many weaknesses and imperfections.[4]

In the covenant of works, Adam was promised a reward for perfect and personal obedience. By contrast, in the covenant of grace, the acceptance and reward of the believer's imperfect obedience is grounded in the *obedience of another*—the perfect and personal obedience of the Mediator. Although the believer's good works are always tainted with imperfections, they are covered with the imputed righteousness and blood of Jesus Christ. A. A. Hodge puts it this way:

> Nevertheless, the good works of sincere believers are, like their persons, in spite of their imperfections, accepted, because of their union with Christ Jesus, and rewarded for his sake. All approaches to God are made through Christ.[5]

---

3. Ibid., 16.6.
4. Ibid.
5. Hodge, *Westminster Confession*, 222.

God's justice is preserved through the imputation of Christ's righteousness; and God's grace is magnified in the acceptance and reward of the believer's imperfect, sincere obedience. Since God's reward of the believer's good works is rooted in the reality of justification by grace alone, it is clear that such an arrangement is evidence of a covenant of grace in contrast to works.

Two Possible Ways of Obtaining Rewards

Reward in the Covenant of Works	Obedience that is Perfect	Obedience that is Personal (from himself)
Reward in the Covenant of Grace	Obedience that is Sincere (of faith), yet Imperfect	Obedience that is Imputed (from another, i.e., Christ)

Fallen Man's Only Option: Reward in the Covenant of Grace

The Republication Paradigm has raised the question of how God rewards human obedience after the fall, particularly in the Mosaic covenant. As we have shown above, there are two distinct ways in which God might grant such a reward: through a covenant of works or through a covenant of grace. Based on the confessional definitions, the only possible way for man to obtain a reward for his obedience after the fall is through a covenant of grace.

After Adam's fall into sin, no one (except Jesus Christ) is able to perform personally perfect good works in order to earn rewards from God through a covenant of works. Since we are wholly dependent on the blood and righteousness of Jesus Christ for God's acceptance of our works[6] how can the imperfect works of fallen sinners or a group of sinners ever merit a reward or blessing? This is why the Confession defines good works in keeping with the redemptive context of the covenant of grace. It makes clear that in the case of believers, "these good works, done in obedience to God's commandments, are the fruits and evidences of a true and lively faith," and that "their ability to do good works is not at all of themselves, but wholly from the Spirit of Christ."[7] In addition, we are told that believers who may "attain to the greatest height which is

6. See WCF 16.6.
7. Ibid., 16.2–3.

possible in this life, are so far from being able to supererogate, and to do more than God requires, as they fall short of much which in duty they are bound to do."[8] Further, "we cannot by our best works merit pardon of sin, or eternal life at the hand of God, by reason of the great disproportion that is between them and glory to come; and the infinite distance that is between us and God." Our works are "defiled, and mixed with weakness and imperfection, that they cannot endure the severity of God's judgment."[9]

Is our inability to merit God's blessing limited to spiritual blessings and the reward of eternal life? In other words, is there room for the idea that man is able to merit some sort of temporal blessing from God? Our Standards answer with an unequivocal, "No!" They state that "in Adam, and by our own sin, we have forfeited our right *to all the outward blessings of this life*, and deserve to be wholly deprived of them by God." Not only have we forfeited all temporal blessings, we are unable to "merit, or by our own industry to procure them."[10]

Thus, the Standards exclude any notion of fallen man obtaining *any* kind of reward through a covenant of works. Man's depraved nature taints any work he might offer to God, thus producing both in his person and in his works a state of absolute demerit. According to the Confession, the nature of the reward to be obtained (whether for salvation or merely temporal blessings) is *wholly irrelevant* in determining whether man's obedience is meritorious. The sinful nature of man (whether viewed individually or collectively as a nation of sinners) necessitates that every reward offered by God and obtained by man be a gift of pure, sovereign grace—and that as the fruit of the covenant of grace.

8. Ibid., 16.4.
9. Ibid., 16.5.
10. WLC 193.

THE REDEFINITION OF GOOD WORKS IN THE REPUBLICATION PARADIGM

In view of the clear teaching of the Reformed creeds, how do advocates of the Klinean republication position account for the reality of man's total inability to merit God's blessing, and at the same time affirm Israel's meritorious obedience? The answer lies in their separation of two layers or levels in the administration of the Mosaic covenant. In a nutshell, the Republication Paradigm applies man's sinful inability to only the eternal blessings of salvation, and reserves Israel's meritorious obedience for the temporal and typological blessings in the promised land.

The Reward for Good Works on the Lower-Foundational Level

First, there is the *lower-foundational level* of God's grace for the individual believer. On this level of the Republication Paradigm, the classic doctrine of the reward for good works appears to be intact when it comes to the individual's works of obedience.

> The need for grateful obedience (the so-called third use of the law) is still there and was there in the old covenant.[11]

On the foundational level of grace, the republication position affirms "the need for grateful obedience," in keeping with the teaching of chapter 16 of the Confession. The law serves on this lower level as a rule of life, and obedience to it is a demonstration of the "fruits and evidences of a true and lively faith."[12] On this level, the Old Testament saint under the Mosaic covenant apparently would recognize that any reward for their good works would come as the fruit of the covenant of grace (just like the New Testament saint).

---

11. Estelle, "Leviticus 18:5," 137.
12. WCF 16.2.

The Reward for Good Works on the Upper-Typological Level

Second, there is the *upper-typological level* which is superimposed on the foundational level of grace in the Republication Paradigm. What is the function of obedience on this temporal, upper-typological level?

> That specific function of obedience has now changed in the New Testament. In this regard, the necessity for obedience plays a somewhat different role under the old covenant. Although the substance of the covenant of grace is the same in both testaments, in the old covenant there was the need for compliance so that this would be the meritorious grounds for Israel's continuance in the land, the typological kingdom.[13]

In the Republication Paradigm, a sharp distinction exists between the national obedience on the upper-typological level and the individual obedience on the foundational level of grace. On this upper-typological level, the traditional Reformed understanding of the believer's good works as wholly incapable of meriting any temporal blessing would have to be suspended. The statement of the Larger Catechism that "in Adam, and by our own sin, we have forfeited our right to all the outward blessings of this life" would simply not apply.[14] How could it, when we are told that Israelites *are able* to merit temporal blessings and by their "own industry to procure them" on this upper typological level? Thus, in the Republication Paradigm, Israel's obedience functions *simultaneously* on two levels—as "there was the need for compliance so that this would be the meritorious grounds for Israel's continuance in the land," while the "need for grateful obedience (the so-called third use of the law) is still there."[15] But does this *dual* function of obedience on two distinct levels of the Mosaic covenant do full justice to the teaching of Scripture as summarized in our Stan-

13. Estelle, "Leviticus 18:5," 136.
14. WLC 193.
15. Estelle, "Leviticus 18:5,"136–37.

dards? In the following section, we will argue that this question must be answered in the negative.

THE UNSTABLE RESULTS OF THE REPUBLICATION PARADIGM

We have seen that the Republication Paradigm redefines what constitutes a good work in its explanation of the "upper-typological level" of the Mosaic covenant. This redefinition is contrary to the traditional Reformed understanding of what constitutes a good work, and inevitably leads to theological instability in the rest of their theological system. As we discuss the instability of the Republication Paradigm with respect to the doctrine of good works and their reward, we will focus our analysis on three key points.

1. The problem of spiritual "schizophrenia" in the life of the Old Testament believer.

2. The problem of a flawed and confusing conception of typology.

3. The instability in the doctrine of sanctification from the inconsistent application of the second and third uses of the law in the life of the New Testament believer.

1. Spiritual Schizophrenia for the Israelite Believer

In the sections above, we have focused on the theological difficulties associated with the Republication Paradigm's combination of works and grace in the two levels of the Mosaic covenant. Proponents of the republication view believe that the separation of the covenant into two levels answers any concerns about the presence of merit in the post-fall world. In their system, merit applies only to temporal blessings and plays absolutely no role in Israel's salvation. Nevertheless, we maintain that the republication construction of the Mosaic covenant not only fails to address these concerns, but also creates additional problems. What do we have in mind?

The basic problem centers on how the *same obedience* of an Israelite in the Republication Paradigm could function on one level to merit a reward (apart from grace) and at the same time on another level be rewarded by grace alone. This dual role of good works leads to a *dualism* in God's people—a kind of spiritual "schizophrenia" in the everyday life of the believer. By this term, we are describing the divided mindset and contradictory approach to life that would result from living according to these opposing views of obedience simultaneously—one of grace and one of works.

The key point is that the personal piety involved in receiving a reward by grace flows from a completely different inner-spiritual mindset than the mindset associated with a reward by meritorious works. A reward by grace is received by one who knows himself to be a wretched sinner, who considers himself unworthy of even the least of God's blessings (see Gen 32:10 KJV). The reception of this kind of reward (by faith) is accompanied by a profound sense of humility, gratitude, and appreciation for having obtained a blessing that he knows could never be earned by his works. To obtain a reward by merit flows out of an entirely different, and opposing, mindset. A reward by merit is obtained by one who believes that he has adequately fulfilled the stipulation of the covenant. It did not require the help of grace, but was performed by one's own power and strength. The reward is thus obtained as wages earned for work completed (see Rom 4:4), rather than as a gift of sovereign grace. Rather than having a sense of unworthiness and gratitude, a reward by merit is accompanied by a sense of entitlement—a reasonable expectation that God will fulfill his half of the bargain and pay what is justly due.

Can the conclusion then be avoided that the Old Testament believer would have possessed such a spiritually divided mindset if—as the Republication Paradigm entails—his obedience functioned simultaneously in two opposing ways in the Mosaic covenant? Would this not have resulted in a life of personal and spiritual confusion and instability? Richard Gaffin (professor emeritus of biblical and systematic theology at WTS, Philadelphia) expresses a similar concern in his review of Michael Horton's *Covenant and Salvation* (Horton is professor of systematic theology and apologetics at WSC, and contributor of *TLNF*). Gaffin comments about the instability that results in the lives of believers in this view of the Mosaic covenant.

> It is difficult for me to see how this way of viewing the theocratic role of Israel as God's covenant people from Moses to Christ (*historia salutis*) avoids creating an uneasy tension, if not polarization, in the lives of his people between grace/faith and (good) works/obedience (*ordo salutis*), especially under the Mosaic economy. As far as I can see from reading the Old Testament, particularly the prophets, the reason Israel went into exile was not failure as a nation to maintain a requisite level of formal obedience to the law in all its details. Rather, Israel lost the land for the deeper reason of *unbelief*, because of the *idolatry* that was at the root of and focused the unbelieving nonremnant's disobedience of God and his law. A further discussion of this issue cannot be entered into here.[16]

The present writers agree that "further discussion" is needed on this important point. Gaffin's concern that the republication paradigm may create an "uneasy tension, if not polarization between grace/faith and (good) works/obedience" is a very real danger.

In fact, according to T. David Gordon, the Republication Paradigm alters the piety of the Israelite under the Mosaic covenant most dramatically. He sets forth the implications of his view that the covenant made at Sinai was "different in kind" from the Abrahamic and new covenants, being "characterized by works, and therefore cursing its recipients and bearing children for slavery."[17]

> If this doesn't sound like any bargain, recall that the original Israelites did not consider it a bargain either, and they resisted Moses' efforts to engage them in it. All

16. Gaffin, review of *Covenant and Salvation*, 146, emphasis in original.

17. Gordon, "Abraham and Sinai Contrasted," 251.

> things considered, many of the first-generation Israelites, who received this covenant while trembling at the foot of a quaking mountain and then wandered in the wilderness, preferred to return to Egypt rather than to enter the covenant with a frightening deity who threatened curse-sanctions upon them if they disobeyed. I do not blame them; their assessment of the matter was judicious and well considered, albeit rebellious. The Sinai covenant administration was no bargain for sinners, and I pity the poor Israelites who suffered under its administration, just as I understand perfectly well why seventy three (nearly half) of their Psalms were laments. I would have resisted this covenant also, had I been there, because such a legal covenant, whose conditions require strict obedience (and threaten severe curse sanctions), is bound to fail if one of the parties to it is a sinful people.[18]

In this statement, we are confronted with an example of how the meritorious works principle within the Republication Paradigm is consistently worked out in one's view of the life of the Old Testament believer. What is striking is the way that Gordon portrays the tangible impact on the piety of God's people under the Republication Paradigm. In his theological system, the "faith" character of the Abrahamic and new covenants is sharply contrasted with the "works" character of the Mosaic covenant. Gordon is right about one thing: the Republication Paradigm's conception of works leads to a very different response from Israel than the one our Confession describes as being common to all the administrations of the covenant of grace.

According to the above characterization of Israel's life, it seems impossible to say under this republication arrangement that believers' good works "manifest their thankfulness, strengthen their assurance, edify their brethren, adorn the profession of the gospel, stop the mouth of adversaries, and glorify God."[19] How is it possible for believers to obey the moral law as "the fruits and evidences of a true and lively faith" whose "ability to do good

18. Ibid.
19. WCF 16.2.

works is not at all of themselves"[20] and at the *same time* render this obedience "as the meritorious grounds for Israel's continuance in the land"?[21] The dual role given to Israel's works in the Republication Paradigm leads to an actual, yet irreconcilable tension in the piety of God's people and in their understanding of the Scriptures.[22] Thus, it is difficult to see how a form of religious and spiritual "schizophrenia" could be avoided in the daily life of an Old Testament believer.

2. Flawed and Confusing Typology

Related to the meritorious nature of temporal-typological blessings in the Republication Paradigm is another concern regarding the conception and use of typology. In the traditional paradigm, the blessings of the land function as a type of the blessing of heaven. Even as the typological blessings were received by grace through faith, so also were the heavenly blessings. Because the type was obtained by grace through faith, Israel learned that the greater blessing of heaven could be obtained in no other way.

In the Republication Paradigm, Israel's meritorious obedience to retain the land is said to serve as a picture and type of Christ's meritorious obedience to obtain salvation. It is unconvincing to say that this view of "typology" would actually serve to drive the Israelites away from their own works and towards the Lord Jesus Christ. The lesson of the typological level may just as easily drive them to their own works and away from Christ (as it did in the case of the Pharisees). Note the disconnect inherent in the

---

20. Ibid., 16.2–3.

21. Estelle, "Leviticus 18:5," 136.

22. For example, it is hard to see how Gordon and the Republication Paradigm accounts for the responses of David and others which are recorded alongside the psalms of lament. Psalms 1, 19 and 119, for example, express humility, gratitude, joy, and love for the perfection of God's law. Such psalms are, in effect, being pitted against the psalms of lament in the above quote. Indeed, if the laments are accounts of the experience of "the poor Israelites who suffered under [the] administration" of a curse-sanctioned covenant of works, one wonders why New Testament believers should sing them at all.

Part 3: The Instability of the Republication Paradigm

Republication Paradigm: If the land is typological of heaven, and the way to blessing in the land is by Israel's own works, how does it follow that God's people will learn that the way to heavenly, eternal blessing is by grace through faith in the work of another? Instead, it would be more consistent with the customary use of typology to say that the Republication Paradigm's principle for obtaining blessing in the land would serve to point the way for obtaining blessing in heaven—by Israel's own meritorious works. If Israel can merit the land by works, why couldn't she merit heaven by works?

Additionally, it is difficult to see how Israel's imperfect obedience can ever be a true type of Christ's perfect obedience. In order for a type to be legitimate, there has to be a degree of correspondence and harmony between the type and the reality. When the essential character of the obedience of Israel is compared with Christ's obedience, by any reasonable assessment, there can be no doubt about the conclusion—namely, a radical disproportion, disharmony, and lack of any real correspondence exists between the two. The difference between them is absolute: the one is imperfect, the other is perfect; the one is fatally flawed, the other is flawless; the one is totally demeritorious, while the other is inherently meritorious. Given the radical difference between the character of Israel's obedience and the obedience of Christ, it is unclear as to how the one can truly serve as a type of the other. In these ways (at least), the typology of the Republication Paradigm is confusing, and flawed in its departure from the nature of biblical typology in the Reformed tradition.[23]

23. On this latter point, see also Cornel Venema's observation that the Republication Paradigm's construction of the Mosaic covenant "begs some important questions regarding the nature of biblical typology" (review of *TLNF*, 90). He goes on to reference Geerhardus Vos and O. Palmer Robertson in their summary of the Reformed view on the relationship between symbols and types. Venema cites Robertson who states: "Vos effectively makes the point that the typological can communicate in its essence nothing different than the symbolized reality it portrays (*Biblical Theology*, 145–46)" (Cited in Venema, review of *TLNF*, 91). As Venema previously stated: "For our purpose, it is important to observe that biblical typology assumes the essential similarity in meaning and symbolism between the Old Testament type and the New Testament reality to which it points forward" (90). In other words, Venema is

3. Instability in Sanctification for the New Testament Believer

Finally, the Republication Paradigm also creates theological instability for some of the traditional Reformed uses of the law. Although it formally affirms them, its meritorious works principle has created an element of theological instability which may detract from the consistent function of the *second* and *third* uses of the law in the life of the believer.

After the fall, one of the uses of God's moral law is to show man his total depravity and inability to do good works and earn God's favor. This *second* use of the law thus serves to point the sinner to Christ and find salvation in him alone. It is difficult to see how the construction of Israel's merit-based probation actually reinforces the law's second use in the republication position. Many proponents of the republication position not only argue that the meritorious works principle was present in the life of the nation of Israel, but also that certain figures (such as Abraham, Noah, and David) actually fulfilled its meritorious stipulations.[24] It is a contradiction to simultaneously argue that the law demonstrates man's total inability to merit, and that certain figures possess the ability to merit. This creates confusion and instability for the second use of the law by contradicting its stated purpose of manifesting man's inability and depravity.

Further, it is also hard to see how the Republication Paradigm avoids creating instability for the *third* use of the law. In the traditional paradigm, one of the "principal uses" of the Mosaic law in the history of redemption was to serve as a binding guide for

---

showing that in order for something to be a type, it must first be a symbol. That is, it must be a real means of grace for the people of God living in the time of its use. Thus, it is difficult to see how Israel's allegedly meritorious obedience in the Republication Paradigm could function as a real means of grace for the people of that period (which is a necessary requirement for traditional, biblical typology). In the nature of the case, a means of grace is governed solely by grace. How can something defined by merit in contrast to grace communicate grace to the one who performs it? Such a notion is illogical.

24. See chap. 5 and appendix 1 in this book.

believers—"as a rule of life informing them of the will of God, and their duty."[25] The exposition of the law in Moses and the Prophets has been understood as addressing, in union with Christ, believers in every age of the covenant of grace. Even the promises and threats attached to the commands (in the old covenant context) were read and applied directly to the life of new covenant believers (Rom 13:8–10; Eph 6:1–3).[26]

However, in the Republication Paradigm, the law given to Israel under Moses has been assigned a different function: to express the republication of a covenant of meritorious works. What has historically served as an expression of the third use of the law, applying to believers in every age, is now viewed as the expression of a meritorious works principle that cannot be applied to believers in the new covenant age. Although the Republication Paradigm formally affirms the third use of the law, it ends up undermining its function. According to the traditional third use of the law, what is required of the believer in the new covenant does not *essentially* differ from what was required of Israel under Moses—namely, sincere obedience, "although accompanied with many weaknesses and imperfections."[27] In keeping with this customary understanding of the law's third use, if the new covenant believer is taught that this kind of obedience from Israel functioned to merit a reward, why shouldn't he conclude that it might merit some kind of reward for him?

This brings us back to the source of the confusion: the redefinition of merit. Simply stated, the Republication Paradigm has defined merit so broadly as to unintentionally include not only the obedience of Christ, Adam, Abraham, Noah, David, and Israel, but also the new covenant saint. If merit simply consists in the fulfillment of the stated stipulations or requirements of the covenant (whatever they may be), what keeps the obedience of new covenant saints from falling under this definition? The new covenant clearly has stipulations. We must believe. We must repent.

25. WCF 19.6.
26. See also WCF 19.5–6.
27. WCF 16.6.

We must show forth the evidence of our faith by our good works. These are the stated requirements of the covenant. Yet, they are the product of God's sovereign grace from beginning to end. Clearly, no proponent of the republication position wants to argue that the New Testament believer's obedience should be construed as meritorious. But with the Republication Paradigm's broad redefinition of merit, it is difficult to see what will prevent the works of new covenant believers from being regarded as meritorious in this system.

CONCLUSION TO PART 3

The present writers believe that it is of vital importance to the church's well being that further consideration be given to the concerns and questions that have been raised about the contemporary Klinean view of republication. In particular, the implications of the redefinition of merit and justice need careful evaluation. This is especially true with respect to the use of the language of "merit" as applied to fallen sinners under the Mosaic covenant. Furthermore, the potential implications of this redefinition of merit in the formulation of the Mosaic covenant need to be addressed with respect to the doctrines of the covenant of works, the covenant of grace, the nature of Christ's merit and satisfaction, the law's uses in sanctification, and even the doctrine of justification. If what we have said above is valid, then what is at stake is not simply a minor concern over an issue which lies at the periphery of Reformed theology. Rather, the republication position is a relatively recent doctrinal paradigm in the history of theology that leads to significant ramifications for the entire Reformed system of doctrine which we all cherish.

CONCLUSION

How the Republication Paradigm Affects the Reformed System of Doctrine

In conclusion, we will rehearse our concerns in summary fashion and seek to demonstrate how the Republication Paradigm disrupts the system of doctrine contained in our Westminster Standards. We will note how the instability of this paradigm changes one's view of God, Adam, the covenants, Christ, and the Old and New Testament believer. Much of what we outline here can be found in fuller detail in parts 2 and 3 of this book. Thus, in order to aid the reader in referring to the fuller exposition of the arguments that undergird this summary, we have provided chapter references at the end of each point. All of these concerns show why we believe that the republication doctrine creates theological instability and, therefore, the church needs to carefully evaluate this doctrinal formulation and consider its repercussions.

THE REPUBLICATION PARADIGM AND THE DOCTRINE OF GOD

Affects God's Transcendence

In the traditional paradigm, God's transcendence is a central concern. This refers to the fact that God is infinitely higher than man in every aspect of his being. This ontological consideration stands behind the clear biblical distinction between the being of God and the being of man. God's being is infinite, eternal and unchangeable. Man's being is finite, temporal and changeable. In the traditional paradigm, God's transcendence is in view at every point in his covenantal transactions with Adam and fallen sinners. The Republication Paradigm compromises God's transcendence by failing to account for the Creator-creature distinction in its definition of the covenant and merit. In the Republication Paradigm, God's transcendence is functionally ignored after God's initial work of creation and does not play any role in defining the way man will attain to the reward of eternal life (chaps. 7, 11).

Affects God's Justice

In the traditional paradigm, God's attribute of justice is grounded in and defined by his holy nature and being. Our standards teach God's justice is absolute and unchangeable.[1] In short, God is by nature "most just, and terrible in his judgments, hating all sin, and . . . will by no means clear the guilty."[2] In the essence of his holiness, God's will is in no way free to change his standard of justice according to the various circumstances of his creatures.

In the Republication Paradigm, God's justice is defined by his mere will: his covenant word is definitive of justice. Thus, God's will is free to change this absolute standard of justice according to the terms of each law covenant. The covenant of works with Adam demands perfect obedience to merit a reward. In the republication

1. See WCF 2.1; WSC 4.
2. WCF 2.1.

of this covenant with Moses, God lowers the requirement by demanding less than perfect obedience to merit an earthly reward. In so doing, the Republication Paradigm has replaced a stable definition of justice with an unstable one. When worked out consistently, this unstable redefinition of justice could have deleterious effects on the doctrine of Justification (chaps. 7, 11).

Affects God's Will

In the covenant of works, God is just to reward Adam if he meets the condition of perfect, personal, and perpetual obedience. In the Republication Paradigm, God is said to be just in the Mosaic covenant to reward Israel if she meets the condition of imperfect obedience. This compromises the will of God because it places God in a position of rewarding a demeritorious work as if it were meritorious. In this paradigm, neither Israel's fallen condition nor the flawed character of her obedience is relevant to the execution of God's justice. In this way, the Republication Paradigm not only creates instability for the doctrine of God's justice, but also for the doctrine of God itself. It does this by allowing God's will to go against his nature, thus placing the two in contradiction to each other (chaps. 7, 11).

THE REPUBLICATION PARADIGM AND THE MERIT OF SINNERS

Allows Human Merit after the Fall

The traditional Augustinian paradigm maintains that merit is impossible for sinners after the fall. The Republication Paradigm teaches that Old Testament figures such as Noah, Abraham, David, and national Israel merited blessings by their works after the fall. The Republication paradigm does this by redefining merit (chap. 5).

Redefines Merit

In the traditional paradigm embodied in the Reformed Confessions, true and proper merit requires at least two things: (1) moral perfection; (2) ontological equality. Further, it distinguishes between "covenant merit" through God's voluntary condescension (for Adam), and "strict merit" based upon the inherent value of one's obedience (for Christ alone). Finally, it categorically and by definition rejects all possibility of merit for sinners (chap. 6).

The Republication Paradigm redefinition of merit results in the rejection of elements of the traditional view. In this new system, merit is simply defined as the fulfillment of the stated stipulations of the covenant (whatever they may be). In other words, it is not defined ontologically, but covenantally. The result is that God can accept less than perfect obedience as meritorious, as long as it is consistent with the stated stipulation of the covenant (chap. 7).

THE REPUBLICATION PARADIGM AND THE DEFINITIONS OF COVENANTS

Rejects Covenant as an Act of Providence

In the traditional paradigm, God's covenants are distinct from creation[3] and are the result of a special act of providence.[4] In the Republication Paradigm, Adam's creation in the image of God means that he is in covenant with God at the moment of creation. This leads to the republication's rejection of voluntary condescension and the redefinition of merit and justice (chaps. 6–7).

Affects the Definition of Covenant of Works

In the traditional paradigm, the covenant of works can only exist when there is a requirement for perfect, personal, and perpetual obedience. This is only possible when man is in a state of sinless

3. See WSC 10.
4. Ibid., 12.

perfection. In the Republication Paradigm, the definition of the covenant of works is changed. Although the covenant of works with Adam requires perfect, personal, and perpetual obedience, the republished "in some sense" covenant of works under Moses requires only sincere imperfect obedience (part 3 introduction and chap. 9).

Affects the Definition of Covenant of Grace

In the traditional paradigm, the requirement of faith and the acceptance of less than perfect obedience was an expression of God's kindness in the covenant of grace. In the Republication Paradigm, God's acceptance of Israel's imperfect sincere obedience is an expression of a works principle. What the traditional paradigm sees as an expression of grace in contrast to works, the Republication Paradigm sees as an expression of works in contrast to grace (chap. 10).

Promotes an Unstable Mixture of Different Types of Covenants

In the traditional paradigm, the covenant of works and the covenant of grace were distinguished in terms of incompatible elements that lay at the core of each. The first was based upon Adam's covenant merit in contrast to grace. The second was based upon God's sovereign grace to the utter exclusion of even the slightest hint of merit. The two covenants are thus by definition incompatible in their very nature. In this way, the traditional paradigm accounted for the principle of the apostle Paul in Romans 11:6: "If it is of grace, it is no more of works. Otherwise, grace would no longer be grace" (chap. 9).

The Republication Paradigm's construction of the Mosaic covenant leaves us with an unstable fusion and mixture of works and grace. Although it seems to affirm that the Mosaic covenant is a covenant of grace, it also describes it in ways that would make it essentially a covenant of works. This calls into question the nature of the contrast between the two covenants, and leads to a blurring of the distinction between works and grace in the Mosaic covenant. As the works-grace distinction is the foundation of the Reformed doctrine of justification, this mixing of grace and works creates instability for this doctrine upon which the church stands or falls (chap. 10).

THE REPUBLICATION PARADIGM AND THE DOCTRINE OF CHRIST

Affects the Uniqueness of the Two Adams

Following the teaching of the apostle Paul, the traditional paradigm sees only two Adam figures in the history of the world. There is a first Adam as well as a second/last Adam (1 Cor 15:45, 47; Rom 5:12ff.). Thus, between the first Adam and the second Adam there are no other true Adam figures. The Republication Paradigm compromises the uniqueness of the two Adams by elevating fallen Israel as a nation to the status of a corporate Adam. In the traditional paradigm, both Adam and Christ were appointed as sinless covenant heads. But fallen Israel is sinful and is thus disqualified from being truly and uniquely analogous to the first or second Adam. In the Republication Paradigm, by elevating Israel to a corporate Adam, the uniqueness of the Savior's most holy and perfect merit is tarnished and diminished by being placed on the same definitional level with the so-called "merit" of sinners (chaps. 8–10).

Compromises the Necessity of Christ's Divine Nature in the Atonement

In the traditional view, Christ's divine nature was essential to understanding the character of his merit. Because Christ was a divine person with a divine nature, he was therefore on equal footing ontologically with God the Father. Whereas Adam in the garden could only merit through God's voluntary condescension (covenant merit), Christ the God-man was able to merit from the intrinsic worth of his obedience (strict merit). Thus, Christ's obedience had an infinite merit and worth, sufficient in itself to atone for the sins of the whole world (chap. 7).[5]

In the Republication Paradigm, it is no longer clear how Christ's divine nature is necessary in determining the character of his meritorious obedience. Merit has been redefined to consist solely in the fulfillment of the stipulation of the covenant divorced from all ontological considerations. Adam's finite nature is of no relevance in determining the character of his potentially meritorious obedience. If ontological considerations are removed, Christ's infinite nature is also no longer relevant in determining the character of his meritorious obedience. In this way, the Republication Paradigm removes a key plank from the traditional understanding of the necessity of Christ's divine nature for his meritorious obedience. One is thus left to find a different answer than Anselm to his famous question, "Why the God-man?" (chaps. 8, 10).

Compromises the Necessity of Christ's Perfect Active Obedience

In the traditional paradigm, merit was defined so as to include an absolute requirement for perfect obedience. This requirement was necessary for merit due to the unchanging character of God's absolute justice. Thus, the necessity of Christ's perfect active obedience was rooted in the definition of merit. By redefining merit so as to no longer require perfect obedience, the republication paradigm has removed the stable foundation for the necessity of Christ's perfect active obedience for our justification. If God is free to accept less than perfect obedience from Israel to merit a reward, why couldn't he be free to accept less than perfect obedience from Christ to merit our salvation? Thus, the republication paradigm's

---

5. See *Canons of Dordt*, head 2, articles 3–4.

redefinition of merit no longer necessitates Christ's perfect active obedience for our justification (chaps. 10–11).

Detracts from Christ's Singular Glory

In the traditional paradigm, Christ's singular glory was brought to the fore in its description of his meritorious obedience. Because he was God, his obedience had an infinite merit and worth far exceeding that which any mere creature (like Adam) could ever perform. Because his obedience was perfect, it had a pristine quality that no fallen sinner or group of sinners (like Israel) could match. In the traditional definition, Christ's "strict merit" was the standard of true and proper merit, Adam's "covenant merit" was far less than Christ's, and Israel's merit was entirely non-existent. In this way, the singular glory of the incomparable obedience of Christ, the God-man, was brought into sharp relief (chaps. 7, 11).

In its redefinition of merit and reformulation of the covenant, the Republication Paradigm has (unwittingly) detracted from Christ's singular glory. Although it acknowledges certain differences between the merit of Adam, Israel, and Christ, the essential definition of merit is the same for all. In order to merit, all one has to do is fulfill the stated stipulation of the covenant. In this way, even fallen sinners are put under a paradigm in which they are able to perform imperfect obedience that can, properly speaking, fall under the definition of merit. This detracts from Christ's singular glory. It does this by ascribing to Adam and especially to fallen, sinful Israel something that can only truly be said of the Lord Jesus Christ. He alone has offered to God an obedience that is truly and properly meritorious. By failing to account for the essential differences between Adam, Israel, and Christ in the definition of merit, the Republication Paradigm flattens them to the same level and in this way detracts from the singular glory of Christ's perfect meritorious obedience (chaps. 8, 11).

Conclusion

THE REPUBLICATION PARADIGM AND THE SPIRITUAL LIFE OF THE BELIEVER

Creates Spiritual Schizophrenia for the Old Testament Israelite

Potential confusion arises when we consider that, under the Republication Paradigm, Israel was simultaneously under two contrary principles of inheritance. Psychologically, it is difficult to see how the ordinary Israelite would sort out this form of typological schizophrenia in his relationship with God. In the Republication Paradigm, the same obedience of corporate Israel functions on the upper level according to a principle of merit and on the lower level according to a principle of grace. The problem for the spiritual life of the believer is that obedience according to these two principles flow from completely opposite mindsets. The mindset of grace is characterized by humility, gratitude, and unworthiness. The mindset of works is characterized by a sense of entitlement demanding the just payment for work performed. Since these two mindsets are in complete contradiction to one another, it is difficult to see how they could coexist in the mind of the ordinary believer under the Mosaic covenant (chap. 12).

Affects Typology

In the traditional paradigm, the blessing of the promised land under Moses functioned as a type and picture of the blessings of heaven. Thus, the way Israel possessed the blessings of the land taught Israel how they were to receive and retain the blessing of heaven. The traditional paradigm insisted that the type and the reality were possessed in the same way: by grace alone through faith alone.

However, the Republication Paradigm insists that the type and reality are possessed in completely opposite ways. Although the reality (heaven) is possessed by grace alone through faith alone, the type (the blessings of the land) is possessed by merit in contrast to grace. This introduces confusion and instability in our conception of biblical typology because it disrupts a key element of continuity between the type and the reality to which it points. If the typological blessings are dependent on meritorious works, why shouldn't the Israelites conclude that the reality of heaven is also obtained in the same way (chap. 12)?

Affects the Second Use of the Law

In the traditional paradigm, the second use of the law refers to its function in convincing fallen man of his sinfulness and inability. Although the republication paradigm formally affirms this use by putting this requirement before national Israel, it actually undermines and confuses it. It does this by arguing that certain Old Testament figures actually did perform obedience that was accepted as meritorious (Noah, Abraham, David, and Israel). It is illogical to say that someone's meriting a reward for less than perfect obedience demonstrates their total inability to merit (chap. 12).

Affects the Third Use of the Law

In the traditional paradigm, one of the "principal uses" of the Mosaic law in the history of redemption was to serve as a binding guide for believers, "as a rule of life informing them of the will of God, and their duty."[6] Israel's obedience under the Mosaic covenant was to be solely an expression of the genuineness and sincerity of the believer's faith in the one true God. As such, it fell under the traditional designation of the third use of the law and was principally identical to the obedience required of new covenant believers.

In the Republication Paradigm, what was once viewed as an expression of the law as a rule of life for believers in every age is now viewed as the expression of a meritorious works principle that cannot be applied to new covenant believers. This creates

6. WCF 19.5–6.

confusion for the New Testament believer when he reads his Old Testament. Do the exhortations and commands in the law of Moses truly apply to him as a rule of life? Large portions of the Law, the Prophets, and the Writings are devoted to the exposition of the Mosaic law for the life of the nation of Israel. Although the Republication Paradigm can formally affirm the third use of the law, it is clear that the Mosaic law—insofar as it expressed the republication works principle—cannot apply to a New Testament believer. In this way, it diminishes the fullness of biblical revelation with respect to the third use of the law and creates an unstable theological basis for its consistent application (chap. 12).

Blurs the Grace-Works Distinction

The traditional paradigm is characterized by the clear distinction between works and grace. Obedience is rewarded according to works only when it is perfect. Obedience is rewarded by grace when it is sincere, albeit imperfect. Thus, any imperfection in a believer's obedience requires that it be rewarded by a principle of grace apart from all merit. In its redefinition of merit, the Republication Paradigm has blurred the distinction between works and grace. The key example is found in the formulation of national Israel's meritorious obedience in the Mosaic covenant. Israel's obedience is by nature sincere, albeit imperfect. Yet it is rewarded on a principle of merit in contrast to grace. The obedience of the new covenant believer is also sincere, albeit imperfect. Yet it is rewarded on a principle of grace in contrast to works. The obedience of Israel and the obedience of the New Testament saint are no different in quality or character (sincere and imperfect), yet each one is rewarded on the basis of contrary principles. In this way, the distinction between works and grace could easily become blurred in the mind of the believer (chaps. 10, 12).

APPENDIX 1

The Kline/*TLNF* Connection

The following quotations show that two of the contributors to *TLNF*, and another colleague at WSC, have explicitly endorsed and are working from Kline's republication doctrine in other writings.

BRYAN ESTELLE

> Did Noah find standing before God, in the sense of getting into heaven or gaining personal salvation, by virtue of his righteousness? By no means! . . . Noah was a sinner. Noah is going to get into heaven only by grace and by means of faith in Christ. He is a son of Adam and as such there can be no communion with God apart from forgiving grace. However, on another level—a typologically instructive level—his family is going to get into the ark by means of his integrity, and his family is going to be delivered from God's wrath. Therefore, Noah is a type of Christ in this sense: by his obedience

he secures[1] deliverance for his family. This is what the exegesis demands, which can be discussed only briefly in this article.[2]

Just as Noah safely delivered his family through that judgment, so also Christ will deliver all those who belong to him through the judgment of God's wrath poured out upon mankind for sin.[3]

What's the point? As Meredith Kline taught, this is an arrangement in which God was pleased to designate the exemplary righteousness of a human being to be a typological signifier of a greater deliverer to come. Another would lead God's family through a greater ordeal of judgment wrath on sin, safe and sound out the other side, so to speak: the coming Messianic Servant-King would win and secure the kingdom for himself and for his people.[4]

---

1. Notice how Estelle's use of "secure" is found in connection to the reference: "as Meredith Kline taught." Kline implies "merit" when he states that Noah's righteousness "is declared to be the ground for granting to him salvation from judgment and inheritance." It is evident that Estelle adopts Kline's understanding of Noah as a type of Christ.

> Noah's exemplary conduct as a covenant servant receives God's approbation and this righteousness of Noah is declared to be the ground for granting to him salvation from judgment and inheritance of the kingdom in the ark . . . And in the case of some of these grantees, including Noah, their righteous acts were the grounds for bestowing kingdom benefits on others closely related to them (cf. Noah's household—Gen 7:1), just as in the case of Christ the many are made righteous by the obedience of the One (Rom 5:19) and become joint-heirs with him of his kingdom inheritance. (Kline, *God, Heaven and Har Magedon*, 79)

2. Estelle, "Noah: A Righteous Man?," 27.
3. Ibid.
4. Ibid.

MICHAEL HORTON

The line from Abraham to his seed runs through David.
While the Sinaitic covenant operates on the principle of
an approximate national fidelity, the Davidic covenant
grows out of the soil of the covenant of promise. You
will recall that a covenant of grant (distinguished from a
suzerainty treaty) is an outright gift or deed of land and
title given in view of past performance, not depending
on present or future accomplishments. Although the
performance of David's heirs does not figure into this at
all (a point emphasized in 1 Sam 7:1–29; 2 Sam 23:1–5;
and Ps 89), the Suzerain makes this royal grant in view
of David's past faithfulness, which even his own present
and future sins cannot annul. In this respect, David is
a type of Christ, who receives his inheritance (covenant
of grant) on the basis of past performance—his victory
over sin and death, and his brother and sisters inherit
his land, title, and riches simply by their union with him
through faith.

The connection between the Abrahamic and Davidic covenants is even more closely established when
we return to Genesis 15:1 and read these words spoken
to Abraham: "Your reward shall be very great." As Kline
points out,

> The term *sakar*, "reward," is used for the com-
> pensation due to those who have conducted a
> military campaign. In Ezekiel 29:19 it refers to
> the spoil of Egypt which the lord gives Nebu-
> chadnezzar as wages for his army (cf. Isa. 40:10;
> 62:11). The imagery of Genesis 15:1 is that of the
> Great King honoring Abraham's notable exhibi-
> tion of compliance with covenant duty by the
> reward of a special grant that would more than
> make up for whatever enrichment he had fore-
> gone at the hands of the king of Sodom for the
> sake of faithfulness to Yahweh, his Lord. [Horton
> inserts endnote 13 (cf. p. 196): Meredith G. Kline,
> *Kingdom Prologue*, vol. 3 (S. Hamilton, MA: self-
> published, 1986), 57.]

Later in the story, God further rewards Abraham's obedience, when he is willing to offer up his son Isaac (Gen. 22:16–18). It is because of Abraham's faithfulness that Isaac and his heirs will now receive the outcome of the promises (Gen. 26:2ff.). Again, this is not the basis of Abraham's salvation, but the means through which that blessing comes to Abraham's heirs. "God was pleased," writes Kline, "to constitute Abraham's exemplary works as the meritorious ground for granting to Israel after the flesh the distinctive role of being formed as the typological kingdom, the matrix from which Christ should come." This does not mean, of course, that his obedience was the ground of his justification before God (which would contradict Genesis 15:6 and its New Testament interpretation) but that it was itself typological of Christ, who would merit by his obedience the reward of everlasting life that this old covenant economy foreshadowed.[5]

DENNIS JOHNSON

On the other hand, it also is true to say that Israel, though small and stubborn, is receiving the land through obedience. Moses has already drawn a connection between obedience and conquest of the Promised Land in Deuteronomy 4:1: "And now, O Israel, listen to the statutes and the rules that I am teaching you, and do them, that you may live, and go in and take possession of the land that the Lord, the God of your fathers, is giving you." Israel is to hear and to do the Lord's commands "that" the promised consequences might follow, namely life and possession of the land. Israel's reception of the relative and temporal/temporary possession of life and land as a reward for relative fidelity to the law of the Lord foreshadows a covenantal principle of reciprocity that the apostle Paul will articulate in its eschatologized, absolutized form: "The one who does [God's commands] shall live by them" (Gal 3:12). But the apostle knows, as

5. Horton, *God of Promise*, 44–45.

one once considered "blameless" under the law but now
gladly trusting in a righteousness not his own (Phil 3:6–
9), that the radical covenant obedience that entitles one
to expect the radical covenant blessing of life in the age
to come is beyond the reach of Adam's fallen children.

Yet, the Pentateuch also shows us that Israel is entering the land not only by grace but also by obedience in
another sense: the Lord's oath to Abraham was in recognition of Abraham's loyalty to the Lord and his covenant.
His heirs' eventual reception of the promised land will
be, in a sense, the Lord's reward for Abraham's fidelity
both in the rescue of Lot (Gen 15:1) and in his willingness to sacrifice his "only" son Isaac (22:16–18; 26:2–5).
M. G. Kline comments concerning Genesis 26:

> Here the significance of Abraham's works cannot
> be limited to their role in validation of his own
> faith. His faithful performance of his covenantal
> duty is here clearly indicated to sustain a causal
> relationship to the blessing of Isaac and Israel. It
> had a meritorious character that procured a re-
> ward enjoyed by others. [Johnson inserts fn. 33:
> M. G. Kline, *Kingdom Prologue: Genesis Founda-
> tions for a Covenantal Worldview* (Overland Park,
> KS: Two Age Press, 2000), 324–25. This edition is
> cited as *Kingdom Prologue* (2000) below.]

Israel, then, would take possession of the land
through obedience—the obedience of another. Kline
elaborates, "Within this typological structure Abraham
emerges as an appointed sign of his promised messianic
seed, the Servant of the Lord, whose fulfillment of his
covenantal mission was the meritorious ground of the
inheritance of the antitypical, eschatological kingdom by
the true, elect Israel of all nations." [Johnson inserts fn.
34: Kline, *Kingdom Prologue* (2000), 325.][6]

---

6. Johnson, *Him We Proclaim*, 298–99.

APPENDIX 2

The Works-Merit Paradigm of Meredith G. Kline

The following quotations are from some of Meredith G. Kline's writings, which give evidence of his "works-merit paradigm" in his doctrine of republication.

> We must keep in mind the typological level of the kingdom that was *secured by Noah's righteousness* if we are to perceive the consistency of the works-grant with the grace principle that was operating at the permanent, fundamental stratum of the Covenant of Grace. The flood judgment was but a type of the messianic judgment and the kingdom in the ark that was *granted to Noah as the reward for his good works* was only typological of the messianic kingdom. Therefore, the covenant of grant to Noah was not in conflict with or an abrogation of the grace of the redemptive covenant that had been revealed to the Sethite community of faith and, of course, continued to be operative in the sphere of eternal realities in the days of Noah and his covenant grant.[7]

> Because of Abraham's obedience redemptive history would take the shape of an Abrahamic kingdom of God

7. Kline, *Kingdom Prologue*, 238–39, emphasis added.

from which salvation's blessings would rise up and flow out to the nations. *God was pleased to constitute Abraham's exemplary works as the meritorious ground* for granting to Israel after the flesh the distinctive role of being formed as the typological kingdom, the matrix from which Christ should come. Within this typological structure Abraham emerges as an appointed sign of his promised messianic seed, the Servant of the Lord, whose fulfillment of his covenantal mission was the meritorious ground of the inheritance of the antitypical, eschatological kingdom by the true, elect Israel of all nations. Certainly, Abraham's works did not have that status. They were, however, accorded by God an analogous kind of value with respect to the typological stage represented by the old covenant. *Though not the ground of the inheritance of heaven, Abraham's obedience was the ground for Israel's inheritance of Canaan.* Salvation would not come because of Abraham's obedience, but because of Abraham's obedience salvation would come to the Abrahamites, the Jews (John 4:22).[8]

In the case of some of these grantees, including Noah, *their righteous acts were the grounds for bestowing kingdom benefits* on others closely related to them . . . , just as in the case of Christ.[9]

Abraham's obedience had typological import. *The Lord constituted it a prophetic sign of that obedience of Christ, which merits the heavenly kingdom for his people. That Abraham's obedience functioned* not only as the authentication of his faith for his personal justification but *as a meritorious performance that earned a reward for others* . . . is confirmed in the Lord's later revelation of the covenant promise to Isaac.[10]

---

8. Ibid., 325, emphasis added.

9. Kline, *God, Heaven and Har Magedon*, 79, emphasis added.

10. Ibid., 102–3, emphasis added.

Abraham, the grantee of the covenant promise. *His exemplary obedience was invested by the Lord with typological significance as the meritorious ground for his descendants' inheritance of the promised land.*[11]

But this [Luke 17:10] *does not mean that human works of obedience are of no merit.* Though we cannot add to God's glory, Scripture instructs us that God has created us for the very purpose of glorifying him. We do so when we reflect back to him his glory, when our godlike righteousness mirrors back his likeness. *Such righteousness God esteems as worthy of his approbation. And that which earns the favor of God earns the blessing in which that favor expresses itself. It is meritorious. It deserves the reward God grants according to his good pleasure.*[12]

Classic covenantalism recognizes that the old Mosaic order (at its foundation level—that is, as a program of individual salvation in Christ) was in continuity with previous and subsequent administrations of the overarching covenant of grace. But it also sees and takes at face value the massive Biblical evidence for a peculiar discontinuity present in the old covenant in the form of *a principle of meritorious works*, operating not as a way of eternal salvation but as the principle governing Israel's retention of its provisional, typological inheritance.[13]

For more, you may access http://sites.google.com/site/themosaiccovenant/Home.

11. Ibid., 127–28, emphasis added.

12. Kline, "Covenant Theology" (unpublished version), para. 11, emphasis added.

13. Kline, "Gospel until the Law," 434, emphasis added.

Bibliography

Augustine. *On the Predestination of the Saints.* In *Nicene and Post-Nicene Fathers*, series 1, edited by Philip Schaff, 5:497–519. Grand Rapids: Eerdmans, 1971.

———. *Confessions.* In *Nicene and Post-Nicene Fathers*, series 1, edited by Philip Schaff, 1:45–207. Grand Rapids: Eerdmans, 1971.

Baugh, S. M. "Galatians 5:1–6 and Personal Obligation: Reflections on Paul and the Law." In *The Law Is Not of Faith: Essays on Works and Grace in the Mosaic Covenant*, edited by Bryan D. Estelle et al., 259–80. Phillipsburg, NJ: P&R, 2009.

Bavinck, Herman. *Reformed Dogmatics.* Vol. 2. Edited by John Bolt. Translated by John Vriend. Grand Rapids: Baker, 2008.

Brown, Michael G., and Zach Keele. *Sacred Bond: Covenant Theology Explored.* Grandville, MI: Reformed Fellowship, 2012.

Calvin, John. "The Lxii Sermon of Iohn Calvin." In *The Sermons of M. Iohn Calvin vpon the Fifth Booke of Moses Called Deuteronomie*, 375–76. London, 1583. https://archive.org/details/sermonsofmiohnca1583calv.

Dennison, James T., Jr. *Reformed Confessions of the 16th and 17th Centuries in English Translation.* Vols. 1–4, 1523–1693. Grand Rapids: Reformation Heritage, 2008–2014.

Dennison, James T., Jr., et al. Review of *The Law Is Not of Faith*, edited by Bryan D. Estelle et al. *Kerux: The Journal of Northwest Theological Seminary* 24 (2009) 3–152. http://www.kerux.com/pdf/Kerux.24.03.pdf.

Engelsma, David J. Review of *Sacred Bond: Covenant Theology Explored*, by Michael G. Brown and Zach Keele. *Protestant Reformed Theological Journal* 46 (2012) 117–22. http://www.prca.org/prtj/Nov2012Issue.pdf.

Estelle, Bryan D. "Leviticus 18:5 and Deuteronomy 30:1–14 in Biblical Theological Developmemt: Entitlement to Heaven Foreclosed and Proffered." In *The Law Is Not of Faith*, edited by Bryan D. Estelle et al., 109–46. Phillipsburg, NJ: P&R, 2009.

———. "Noah: A Righteous Man?" *Modern Reformation* 19 (2010) 27. http://read.uberflip.com/i/16716/28.

Bibliography

Estelle, Bryan D., et al., eds. *The Law Is Not of Faith: Essays on Works and Grace in the Mosaic Covenant*. Phillipsburg, NJ: P&R, 2009.

Gaffin, Richard B., Jr. Review of *Covenant and Salvation: Union with Christ*, by Michael S. Horton. *Ordained Servant* 18 (2009) 145–49. http://www.opc. org/OS/Ordained_Servant_2009.pdf.

Gordon, T. David. "Abraham and Sinai Contrasted in Galatians 3:6–14." In *The Law Is Not of Faith: Essays on Works and Grace in the Mosaic Covenant*, edited by Bryan D. Estelle et al., 240–58. Phillipsburg, NJ: P&R, 2009.

Hodge, A. A. *Outlines of Theology: For Students and Laymen*. 1860. Reprint, Grand Rapids: Zondervan, 1991.

——. *The Westminster Confession of Faith: A Handbook of Christian Doctrine Expounding the Westminster Confession*. 1869. Reprint, Carlisle, PA: Banner of Truth, 1992.

Horton, Michael. *God of Promise: Introducing Covenant Theology*. Grand Rapids: Baker, 2006.

Irons, Lee. "Redefining Merit." In *Creator, Redeemer, Consummator: A Festschrift for Meredith G. Kline*, edited by Howard Griffith and John R. Muether, 253–69. Jackson, MS: Reformed Academic, 2000.

Johnson, Dennis E. *Him We Proclaim: Preaching Christ from All the Scriptures*. Phillipsburg, NJ: P&R, 2007.

Jones, Mark. Review of *The Law Is Not of Faith: Essays on Works and Grace in the Mosaic Covenant*, edited by Bryan D. Estelle et al. *Ordained Servant* 19 (2010) 115–20. http://www.opc.org/OS/Ordained_Servant_2010.pdf.

Kline, Meredith G. "Covenant Theology Under Attack." *New Horizons Online* (1994) no pages. http://www.opc.org/new_horizons/Kline_cov_theo. html.

——. "Covenant Theology Under Attack." Unedited version, 1994. No pages. http://upper-register.com/papers/ct_under_attack.html.

——. *God, Heaven and Har Magedon: A Covenantal Tale of Cosmos and Telos*. Eugene, OR: Wipf & Stock, 2006.

——. "Gospel until the Law: Rom 5:13–14 and the Old Covenant." *Journal of the Evangelical Theological Society* 34 (1991) 433–46.

——. *Kingdom Prologue: Genesis Foundations for a Covenantal Worldview*. Eugene, OR: Wipf & Stock, 2006.

McGrath, Alister. *Iustitia Dei: A History of the Christian Doctrine of Justification*. Vol. 1. Cambridge: Cambridge University Press, 1986.

Murray, Ian H. *The Life of John Murray*. Carlisle, PA: Banner of Truth, 2007.

Murray, John. *Collected Writings of John Murray*. Vols. 2 & 4. Carlisle, PA: Banner of Truth, 1977/1982.

——. *Covenant of Grace: A Biblico-Theological Study*. London: Tyndale, 1954.

——. *The Imputation of Adam's Sin*. Phillipsburg, NJ: P&R, 1959.

——. *Principles of Conduct*. Grand Rapids: Eerdmans, 1957.

Orthodox Presbyterian Church. *Report on Justification: Presented to the Seventy-Third General Assembly of the Orthodox Presbyterian Church*.

Willow Grove, PA: Committee on Christian Education of the Orthodox Presbyterian Church, 2007. http://www.opc.org/GA/justification.pdf.

Ramsey, D. Patrick. "In Defense of Moses: A Confessional Critique of Kline and Karlberg." *Westminster Theological Journal* 66 (2004) 373–400. https://sites.google.com/site/mosaiccovenant/reading.

Shepherd, Norman. *The Call of Grace: How the Covenant Illuminates Salvation and Evangelism.* Phillipsburg, NJ: P&R, 2000.

———. "The Need to Persevere (II)." *Outlook* 42 (1992) 20–21.

———. "Law and Gospel in Covenantal Perspective." Self-published pamphlet, 2004.

———. *The Way of Righteousness: Justification Beginning with James.* LaGrange, CA: Kerygma, 2009.

Strimple, Robert B. Doctrine of Christ syllabus. Class notes from the Doctrine of Christ course, taught at WTS California, 1992.

———. "Westminster Confession of Faith: Was the Mosaic Covenant a Republication of the Covenant of Works?" Unpublished essay. https://sites.google.com/site/mosaiccovenant/reading.

Turretin, Francis. *Institutes of Elenctic Theology.* Vol. 2. Edited by James T. Dennison Jr. Translated by George Musgrave Giger. Phillipsburg, NJ: P&R, 1994.

VanDrunen, David. "Israel's Recapitulation of Adam's Probation under the Law of Moses." *Westminster Theological Journal* 73 (2011) 303–24. https://sites.google.com/site/mosaiccovenant/reading.

———. "Natural Law and the Works Principle Under Adam and Moses." In *The Law Is Not of Faith,* edited by Bryan D. Estelle et al., 283–314. Phillipsburg, NJ: P&R, 2009.

Venema, Cornelis. Review of *The Call of Grace,* by Norman Shepherd. *Mid-America Journal of Theology* 13 (2002) 232–48.

———. Review of *The Law Is Not of Faith,* edited by Bryan D. Estelle et al. *Mid-America Journal of Theology* 21 (2010) 35–101. https://sites.google.com/site/mosaiccovenant/reading.